11/99

Do You Believe
in Ghosts?

Do You Believe in Ghosts?

John G. Sutton
Illustrated by Sarah Warburton

ELEMENT
CHILDREN'S BOOKS

SHAFTESBURY, DORSET · BOSTON, MASSACHUSETTS · MELBOURNE, VICTORIA

Contents

This book is dedicated, with all my love,
to my dear daughter Dulcie Jane and her husband
Robert John Dowrick

© Element Children's Books 1999
Text © John G. Sutton 1999
Illustrations © Sarah Warburton 1999

First published in Great Britain in 1999 by
Element Children's Books
Shaftesbury, Dorset SP7 8BP

Published in the USA in 1999 by
Element Books, Inc.
160 North Washington Street,
Boston MA 02114

Published in Australia in 1999 by
Element Books and distributed by
Penguin Australia Limited,
487 Maroondah Highway, Ringwood,
Victoria 3134

Cover design by The Design Group
Typeset by Dorchester Typesetting Group Ltd.
Printed and bound in Great Britain by
Creative Print and Design Wales, Ebbw Vale
British Library Cataloguing in Publication data available.
Library of Congress Cataloging in Publication data available.

ISBN 1 901881 49 0

Acknowledgements

Mrs. Lois J. Barin, M.A., Ohio State University, Columbus, Ohio, U.S.A. The author wishes to thank Mrs. Barin (Queen of the Crits) for reading and commenting on the text in draft.

Mr. Derek Acorah, psychic medium, Liverpool, Merseyside, England. The author wishes to thank Mr. Acorah for his psychic input into the research.

Dr. Larry Montz, Ph.D., the International Society for Paranormal Research, P.O. Box 291159, Los Angeles, California 90027, U.S.A. www.ispr.net. The author wishes to thank Dr. Montz and his team at the ISPR for their help with the technical research and for sight of the ISPR files.

Mr. Ray Taylor, B.A., Editor, *Psychic World*, P.O. Box 14, Greenford, UB6 OUF, U.K. For research facilities through the monthly journal *Psychic World*.

Ms. Alexandra Walker, D.A., A.M.A., and Mr. Stephen Whittle, Museum and Art Officers at the Harris Museum, Preston, Lancashire, U.K., and the Directors of Heart of the North Limited (Whistling Past the Graveyard Exhibition) for permission to photograph the screaming skull of Slaithwaite.

Mrs. Mary Sutton, the Office, Clayton-le-Woods, Leyland, Preston, England. For her services above and beyond the call of duty.

Joe Cooper, M.Sc., B.Sc. (Econ.), Headingley, Leeds, U.K. For wearing the wrinkliest shirt in the world and being an all-round good guy.

Introduction

Have you ever wondered whether ghosts are for real? Do the dark shadows hide spooks and spirits? Perhaps you don't believe in such things, but I do. Since I'm the author of this book you would expect me to say that, but I have seen ghosts with my own eyes. I have heard spirits speak, and trembled as invisible hands tweaked my toes as I tried to sleep.

Of course many people think you have to be nuts to believe in ghosts and ghouls. But if you had seen what I have seen, then maybe you too would believe in the weird world of the spook.

This book contains many true-life stories about people who have seen ghosts. You can decide whether or not you think these tales of terror are true. To help you do this, there's a simple multiple-choice quiz at the end of each tale.

You just select the answer that most closely matches your opinion and, when you have read all the strange stories, total up your selections and look at the final assessment at the end.

There are also tests for you to do with your family and friends. If you want to go on your own spook hunt, we have some tips from the professionals, and I have devised a safe and simple to follow step-by-step guide to hunting ghosts. You might even get a photograph of one, who knows?

Throughout this book you will find many strange stories and some that are quite scary. During my research I had to go to many haunted houses and was frightened more than once. The very scariest thing I did was meeting the screaming skull of Slaithwaite face to bone. That story and many others are here to help you decide if you really do believe in ghosts and ghouls.

There is no need to be afraid …honest!

John G. Sutton

Chapter 1

Spook Quiz

Think you know all about ghosts and spooky stuff? Put your knowledge to the test before reading this book.

You can check again afterwards, to see if you've learned something – that's if you're not too scared!

1) What is the name given to a person who scares ghosts away?

a) Father. b) Exorcist. c) Spookbuster.

2) Which dead American president is said to haunt the White House?

a) Kennedy. b) Nixon. c) Lincoln.

3) What is the date of Halloween?

a) May 1. b) October 31.
c) February 2.

4) What can knocking noises signify?

a) A spirit trying to communicate.
b) Engine trouble. c) Neighbors banging on the wall – turn that music down!

5) What is a medium?

a) A size below large. b) A psychic person.
c) A musical instrument.

6) What is a pentagram?

a) A three-wheeled cycle. b) A magic circle.
c) A five-pointed star.

7) What is a poltergeist?

a) A noisy spirit. b) A German turkey.
c) A strong Polish spirit.

8) What do the initials ESP stand for?

a) Exit secondary program. b) Extrasensory
perception. c) Eastern superpowers.

9) What is a séance?

a) A popular Irish dance. b) A ghostly ant.
c) A group meeting trying to contact spirits.

10) What is a ghoul?

a) A waterproof coat. b) An evil ghost or
spirit. c) A howling ghostly wolf.

Spook quiz answers

**1) b 2) c 3) b 4) a 5) b 6) c 7) a 8) b
9) c 10) b**

Your spook quiz assessment

8-10 correct:
Spookily well informed!

4-7 correct:
Not bad for starters.

0-3 correct:
You're not taking this seriously, are you?

What is a Ghost?

The traditional ghost has his head tucked underneath his arm as he walks through an ancient castle. This is the way many think of ghosts – as lost souls forever wandering the dark halls and grim dungeons where they met their end.

Of course not all ghosts look the same. Some look much as they did when they were alive. Others are seen as bright white lights floating mysteriously through the air. Many are sensed more than seen, as when you feel an unseen hand stroking your hair in the dark. Others produce scents or smells that were often around them when they lived on Earth. For example, the ghost of a pipe smoker might smell of tobacco, and a ghostly florist of flowers. Then there are playful spirits that move objects or make electrical equipment fail. There are many ways in which ghosts can appear and each, just like us, will have their own way of doing things.

Many people think that ghostly visions take place only in the mind of the person who experiences them. There are many things we don't know about how the human brain works. Certainly the mind can play tricks. There is also a tendency for people to see what they expect to see, which some say accounts for reports of mass sightings of strange phenomena.

Others believe that ghosts are the spirits or life energy of humans or animals who have died. Some believe that the shock of being brutally killed causes the spirit of the victim to leave the physical body before it is prepared for eternity, becoming trapped forever in a kind of twilight zone between this world and the next. Such spirits endlessly tread their weary way round and round the area of their death. The spirits of murderers are also said to haunt the scenes where, in life, they committed their horrible crimes.

Some scientific researchers into haunted houses believe that many ghostly sightings are really a kind of projection of images somehow recorded in the walls or the atmosphere. These ghosts always repeat their actions. It has been suggested that very damp places are most likely to trap and record highly emotional events. This could explain the sightings of American Civil War soldiers re-enacting their battles on the foggy fields where they were killed. Or the ghostly legions of Roman soldiers said to march through the ancient streets of the city of York in England. The argument is that they are not ghosts at all, just recordings of the past playing back like an old video film.

Throughout the history of humankind there have been tales of ghosts. Shakespeare, the great British dramatist and poet, wrote about ghostly visitations. The Bible is full of references to ghosts and spirits. Every country in the world has its own ghost stories. And the belief that life continues after death is common to most religions. This spirit life is said to go on in the "next world." It is from this next world that ghosts in their truest form are thought to appear.

There are good and bad people, and perhaps, after death, they turn into good and bad spirits.

When these spirits show themselves to us, we see ghosts. From good spirits expect goodness, help, and joy. From bad spirits – well, we'll come to that later in the book.

Just remember, there is no need to be afraid. If you are in any way scared, then put this book down and go and talk to a parent, teacher, or guardian. You may also wish to seek guidance from your religious instructors. This is a sensible thing to do. However, it is you who must decide what you believe. Not everything that goes bump in the night is a ghost, so keep your spirits up!

Chapter 3

Spooks' A–Z Identity Parade

angel

A winged being in human shape, generally shining white. In some religions angels are thought to be messengers of God.

apparition

Another word for a visible ghost.

ghost

The spirit of a person or an animal making itself seen or sensed by the living. Ghosts can appear to be solid or as filmy white mists.

ghoul

An invisible ghost that is evil in nature and feeds on the life energy of its human victims.

guardian angel

A shining spirit that is thought to protect just one individual. There is a belief that we all have guardian angels, at least one each, and more if they work shifts.

haunting

The repeated appearance of a ghost in a specific area, or any recurring weird phenomena taken to be supernatural.

phantom

A seemingly solid apparition or ghost.

poltergeist

A noisy ghost that can be very destructive and hurtful. These are usually invisible.

Poltergeists are reported to break things, throw pots and pans across rooms, and even to lift objects so that they float in midair. They bite, nip, and generally cause mayhem. Many strange things can happen when poltergeists enter a home. Some think there is a scientific explanation for these phenomena, and that they are involuntarily caused by young people. Perhaps you know the feeling!

screaming skull

A human skull that is supposed to be haunted by the spirit of its original owner.

soul

A part of a person – their higher nature – that has no outward physical reality and is believed by many to live on in some way after death. The definition of soul differs from one religion to another.

spirit

Similar to soul. A supernatural entity that is alive but has no physical body.

spook

A catch-all term for any type of ghost.

the White Lady, or woman in white

A female apparition, usually described as being bathed in light. She often speaks to those who see her, mainly children.

There are reports of the White Lady appearing as far away as China, but it is more common in areas where Christianity is dominant, and the White Lady is often taken to be the Virgin Mary. The White Lady usually issues warnings of disasters to come, though these are often given as secrets, or the details are too vague to be of any help.

I once encountered the Lady in White; it happened in early December 1968 at the army barracks in the little German town of Sennelager on the outskirts of Paderborn. I had been in bed with a serious case of flu, unable to eat for days because I was so ill. I gradually became very weak. Then one night I awoke to find myself walking towards the little Lancashire village in England where I was born.

I could see the signpost for Foulridge, my home village, ahead of me, but I was too tired to walk any further. My feet felt as though they were made of lead. Then a lady dressed all in white came to me and held out her hand.

"You have a choice," she said. "Do you want to continue on your journey or return to your body?"

I could feel a sense of pure love surrounding her like a golden glow. Reaching out, I took her hand and replied, "I must return to my body."

When I opened my eyes I was back in the barrack block in Germany and my illness had gone. Within days I was fully fit.

Since that day I have often wondered what would have happened if I had chosen to walk on to the village of my birth. Perhaps I would never have woken again and you would never have read this book.

A Ghostly Soldier of the American Civil War

During the American Civil War (1861-65) there were many battles fought in and around the little town of Beebe, Arkansas. Al Collier and his wife Karen live there now with their pet dog Lady, a black Labrador and cocker-spaniel cross. Their house stands along a highway which was called Campground Road during the war. Along this road tramped many Confederate soldiers, known as Johnny Rebs. They were seeking medical help at one of the two nearby military hospitals, Camp Nelson, 10 miles to the south, and a converted Episcopal church at Little Rock, a further 20 miles away.

There is a memorial on the site of Camp Nelson, erected to honor those who fell in the conflict between the Northern and Southern states of the U.S.A. It is believed that over 1,800 men are buried in unmarked mass graves thereabouts. Al Collier and Lady the dog know that not all rest in peace.

Johnny Reb

It was a warm night in July 1996. Outside the Colliers' home, Campground Road was a silent highway, shimmering in the moon's silver light. Around half past two in the morning Al was woken by the barking of Lady. At first he thought there might be a burglar, or some lost soul on the lonely road.

Al hurried downstairs to see what was wrong. On opening the door he saw nothing out of the ordinary. There was no one there except Lady. She was barking at an old pecan tree on the other side of a field of dry grass. This tree had stood for perhaps two hundred years, providing a shady spot where travelers could rest during the heat of the day. Lady ran up to it and sat with her back pressed against the trunk of the tree. She had stopped barking. As he watched, Al saw a mist begin to form. Within its clouds he made out the shape of a man.

Gradually the figure of the man became clear. On his head was a soldier's hat with a faded badge at the front. He was dressed in a pair of ragged gray Confederate army trousers and his torn shirt was hanging loose and open at the neck. His feet were bare and filthy from the long

dusty road. Across his body his right hand clasped his obviously injured left, which was wrapped in a dirty red bandanna. This soldier was seriously wounded and he looked close to death.

The figure approached the pecan tree and sat down alongside the dog. After a moment he reached out and stroked Lady's ears. The dog did not move. She just stared silently up at the haunted eyes of this long-dead soldier.

Al stood transfixed in the moonlight, watching this eerie scene. Was Lady in any danger? Then he heard the spirit of the soldier speak to him in a broad Southern drawl. "Sure is a fine animal," said the ghost. "Bet she's a good hunting dog."

The soldier seemed at ease, resting against the tree. Al listened as he told his story. "Gun blew up in my hand. I got the poison in it. I was trying to get to the field hospital at Camp Nelson." A faint half-smile flickered across his old young face.

As if he could read Al's mind, the ghost spoke again. "I died here," he said. "Right here in the cool shade of this tree. It was such a peaceful place to die, sometimes I come back. I was only a boy of twenty years. They called me Josh then. I was born in Memphis, Tennessee."

As he told Al the sad story of his short life, Lady curled close to the phantom of that Confederate soldier as if to comfort him. "Take care, girl," he said, gently stroking the dog. Softly and ever so slowly, the outline of the ghostly soldier began to fade, and Lady was left alone in the moonbeams and shadows under the pecan tree. Only a thin mist drifted westwards into the sky.

Summer mist

Since that night Al and Lady often stand at the door of their house and gaze out on moonlit evenings across the dry grass field to that old pecan tree. Sometimes, in the swirls of summer mist, they seem to see the sad figure of a long-dead Johnny Reb. He stops to rest under the tree, on his way to a hospital he will never reach, and eternity.

ASSESSMENT

 **Q: What do you think really happened under the pecan tree?**
A) Nothing. The description of the soldier sounds more like something seen in the movies than at night from a distance.

B) The dog behaved strangely, and Al Collier's imagination was sparked by the mist and the moonlight.

C) I think the ghost of the soldier returns to the pecan tree because that was where he died peacefully a long time ago.

Chapter 5

Rocky: The Cat That Came Back

The Breckenfield family live in a beautiful house by Lake Geneva in Switzerland. They had always wanted to own a parrot but were worried that their pet cat Rocky might not like it.

One day Mrs. Carol Breckenfield heard about a poorly Amazon gray parrot that had been mistreated by its owners. The poor creature had been left outside too long in the cold and had lost two claws to frostbite. When she went to see it, Carol decided there and then to look after this lovely but injured parrot. Carol named the parrot Moki, and she took it home with her. She just hoped Rocky the cat wouldn't mind.

Moki talks

After a few months Moki learned to trust everyone in the Breckenfield home, including the cat. He would sit on his open perch next to his cage, nibbling bits of banana and squawking in delight whenever Rocky came into the room. Soon Moki began to talk, which was a sure sign that he was now a happy parrot.

Moki learned the names of all the Breckenfield family and called them out correctly. Each time Carol entered the room where he sat, Moki would shout, "Hi, Carol! What are you doing?" in his funny, squawky parrot voice.

Moki even learned the name of the cat, and it was

23

great fun for the Breckenfield family to watch these two "talking" to each other. Rocky, who was a big, huggable Persian pussy, would wander in from his adventures and softly meow a little hello to Moki. Then he would stretch out on his favorite sofa and listen to the parrot chattering to him. "You OK, Rocky?" Moki would say, or "Hi, Rocky! What are you doing?" The cat seemed to know that this parrot was his friend and whenever he meowed, Moki would talk to him.

As time passed, they became inseparable buddies. Rocky would often be found asleep next to the parrot's cage. It was as though the cat were protecting his feathered friend.

Rocky's return

Then one day Rocky suddenly became ill. Carol took her beloved cat to the vet's clinic, but he could not be saved. That same afternoon Rocky died. Everyone in the Breckenfield house cried, and even Moki looked sad. For days and days the parrot uttered not a word.

Some weeks after Rocky's death, Carol was sitting at the table in the living room opposite Moki's cage when she heard the parrot speak. "Hi, Rocky," said the bird. "Are you OK?"

Out of the corner of her eye Carol is certain she saw what looked like her old Persian cat. Moki was standing on his perch staring hard at the center cushion of the sofa, exactly where Rocky used to sit.

Carol searched the room, thinking that perhaps a stray cat had got in and Moki had mistaken it for Rocky, but no cat did she find.

Some days later Carol's daughter Cindy thought she saw Rocky's ghost. She knew the cat was dead, yet she saw the creature quite clearly and watched it jump up on the sofa next to Moki's perch.

"Are you OK, Rocky?" said the parrot, looking directly at his friend.

The ghostly cat meowed his usual hello. Then, before Cindy's astonished eyes, the image of Rocky began to fade. Slowly the seemingly solid form of the cat became transparent and soon it had completely vanished.

Cindy told her mother, who decided to report the spooky experience to Mr. Breckenfield. When they did so, both Carol and Cindy were shocked to learn that he too had seen the ghost of Rocky. "I didn't want to say anything," he said, "because you might have thought I was making it up."

Moki the parrot is not worried what anyone thinks. He can often be heard chattering away to his never for-gotten friend. "Hi, Rocky, are you OK?" he says to what seems to be just an empty cushion. But to Moki that sofa contains the ghost of Rocky, the cat that came back.

ASSESSMENT

Q: Why do you think Moki the parrot says "Hi, Rocky"?

A) Parrots repeat phrases they have learned, without understanding their meaning. Humans try to make the random speech imitations fit the circumstances.

B) I think the parrot may be missing his friend Rocky and says the words he knows, hoping his friend will come back.

C) Moki can see the ghost of Rocky and is talking to his friend.

Chapter 6

Famous American Ghosts

Abraham Lincoln

The United States of America has many famous ghosts. These include the spirit of the assassinated President Lincoln, who is said to haunt the White House. His ghost has been seen by many people, among them the wife of Calvin Coolidge when she was First Lady in the 1920s. The spirit has been described as having a deeply furrowed face and walks with a shambling gait.

Others who have seen the ghost include Queen Wilhelmina of the Netherlands. She was sleeping in the Rose Room of the White House when someone knocked at the door. When she opened it, she saw the ghost of Lincoln staring at her with deep, dark eyes.

Even the great British war leader Winston Churchill was afraid of the ghost. He refused to sleep in the Rose Room and insisted on being moved. In more recent times Maureen Reagan, the daughter of ex-President Ronald Reagan, has reported seeing Lincoln's ghost.

After his assassination in 1865, President Lincoln's body was transported by train from Washington, D.C., to his home town of Springfield, Illinois. At each station on the way the train bearing Lincoln's body halted for eight minutes, giving people a chance to pay their last respects. According to legend, every year on April 14, the anniversary of his murder, a ghost train travels the same route. They say it stops at each station for exactly eight minutes, just as the funeral train did.

The haunted bridge

The Sunshine Skyway Bridge at Tampa Bay, Florida, was the scene of a series of strange shipping accidents in 1980. These caused the loss of over fifty lives in a five-month period.

According to local legend, the bridge is haunted by the ghost of a construction worker who was killed building the bridge. It seems he slipped and fell into the wet cement of one of the bridge's supports and was built into the structure.

There are those who say that the spirit is returning to cause accidents in revenge for that horrible and untimely death. Skeptics point out that there is no concrete proof whatsoever.

The gray ghost

In the city of Seattle, Washington, there is a section known as "old Seattle." This part of the city is reputed to be haunted by many ghosts.

In the area of Pioneer Square stand the rotting remains of an abandoned underground shopping complex. Within its dark and cobwebbed tunnels, there have been many sightings of a ghostly gray man. He is believed to have been employed in the city bank and it is next to the old vault that his spirit is seen. Local legend has it that this man so loved his work that even in death he returns to guard the money.

Many tourists who visit the site have reported seeing the gray man. Today the old tunnels are quite an attraction, for living visitors as well as the spooky kind.

The Bell Witch

The Bell Witch of Tennessee is one of America's best-known hauntings. This spook even got the better of the famous army general Andrew Jackson, later to become the seventh US president.

The phantoms began to appear in the year 1817, when John Bell and his family were living on a farm near Adams in the state of Tennessee. One day John saw a huge black dog with eyes of fire. In terror he fired his shotgun at it. This had no effect on the hound whatsoever, and convinced him that it must be a supernatural being.

Shortly afterwards John Bell saw a giant turkeylike creature that was bigger than he was. He took one look at the spooky bird and ran.

The haunting got worse. The spirit must have followed John Bell home to his farmhouse, because soon other members of his family were subjected to some really rotten ghostly tricks. They were not alone. In fact, the area for miles around was said to be haunted by what became known as the Bell Witch.

When General Jackson was driving to the farm in a coach, bringing an exorcist to cleanse the place of the evil spirit, some unseen force stopped the horses and they refused to move. It had to be the Bell Witch. The General even heard the witch's voice. She threatened to show herself. But somehow he pressed on and reached the farm.

That night terrible things happened in the Bell farm. A wicked-sounding voice screamed from empty air: "I have lived a million years!" Invisible hands dragged bedclothes away from the terrified occupants bravely trying to sleep. Then the exorcist was severely beaten about the head by an unseen attacker. In blind terror he fired a gun loaded with a silver bullet, but the Bell Witch only laughed. Fearing for his immortal soul, the exorcist dashed from the Bell farm and ran screaming into the night.

Things really got nasty after the General left. Strong invisible hands would pinch and nip the occupants of the Bell farm. Betsy Bell, the twelve-year-old daughter of the family, was attacked by the ghostly witch, and pins were pushed into her body. Vile voices from unseen ghosts shouted rude words and curses all over the house.

Threats against the life of John Bell were also heard.

And, after years of torment, he died a horrible death. On the night he died, the Bell Witch was heard to cackle with glee.

The witch must have been able to see the future, for it is said that a croaking voice from nowhere predicted the American Civil War and the two world wars. We do not know what else she predicted.

The area around the old Bell farm near Adams, Tennessee, is still said to be haunted.

Mysterious knocking from the world beyond

In the year 1848, three sisters – Margaretta, Kate, and Leah Fox – were at the center of a famous poltergeist case. The sisters lived with their parents in Hydesville, in the state of New York, U.S.A. They reported hearing a series of knocks and rappings that seemed to come out of thin air.

The sisters wanted to communicate with the invisible being that was making the sounds. They invented a code based on the number of raps, starting with one knock for Yes and two for No.

When they spelled out what the knocks were saying, the message was that a traveling salesman visiting the house years before had been murdered there.

Subsequent digging in the earth of the cellar below the house uncovered human remains and also a tin box of the kind that salesmen used to carry their samples in.

The Fox sisters are credited with starting the belief in spirit communication.

The phantom hitchhiker

The city of Chicago, Illinois, has one of the most scary of all modern spooks, a ghostly hitchhiker. Resurrection Mary, as she is known, is supposed to be the spirit of a young woman killed in a car accident in 1934. For it is since that date that her phantom has been seen standing by the roadside seeking a lift to the graveyard in the area known as Justice in the suburbs of Chicago. She is said to be very pale with icy cold skin.

Many motorists have reported giving this ghostly hitchhiker a ride. Most say she asks them to stop on Archer Avenue, where she gets out and walks into the cemetery, through locked and bolted gates. Some motorists say she vanishes as their cars pass along Archer Avenue. There are those who have seen the ghost staring out through the rusty iron railings that surround the cemetery.

Sightings of Resurrection Mary increased during the mid-1970s, when the old graveyard was being renovated. The cemetery on Archer Avenue, Justice, Chicago, is there to this day, and many believe that so is Resurrection Mary.

Chapter 7

What to Do in Case of Haunting

1) Run!

2) Report exactly what you have seen to one of your parents, guardians, or teachers.

3) Stay away from the area where you thought you saw the spook until your parents or other sensible adults say it is OK to return.

4) Use some form of magical self-protection. Clear this with your parents or guardians first! Here are some ways you can keep spooks away from you, your home, and your family.

a) If you are religious, say your prayers every night and believe that God will keep you safe from harm. This is the very best form of protection.

b) Draw a five-pointed star, or pentagram, around your bed. You could use chalk to do this. Spooks are supposed to be unable to cross into a pentagram.

c) Evil spirits do not like religious objects. If you are a Christian, for example, place a Palm Sunday palm-leaf cross near the front door of your house.

d) The herb rosemary is believed to protect houses from evil spooks. Place some near the front and rear entrances to your home. You can also put some of this herb in a muslin cloth and keep it under your pillow.

e) Mirrors are thought to reflect evil. Placing a mirror near a door could frighten away spooks: they get scared by their own horrible appearance.

f) Salt is believed to protect against evil spirits. Sprinkle it around the outside of your home. Some say you should mix it with water first.

g) Iron is a strong protection against spooks, who are thought to be very scared of this metal. A good way to use iron as protection is to hang a horseshoe over all the outer doors of your home. The shoe must be hung with the open end upward to hold in good luck.

h) Tea leaves scattered in front of a house are thought to keep ghosts away.

i) Scissors open on a table near the front door of a house are thought to drive away witches and evil spirits.

j) The rowan tree is also said to have the power of scaring evil spirits away. The red berries of this tree may be worn as a necklace.

k) Pins – ordinary sharp little metal pins – stuck into the door of a house are thought to keep out any evil spirit trying to enter.

l) Onions, uncut and unpeeled, placed at a window or door protect against spooks.

m) Oak leaves fixed above your bed protect against ghosts in the night.

n) Nails, especially old rusty nails, carried in the pocket are a good charm against spooks.

o) A four-leaf clover in your pajama pocket is said to help you sleep undisturbed by evil spirits.

p) Birch twigs worn or carried in the pocket are thought to repel bad luck and unwanted ghosts.

q) Black beans were used by the ancient Romans to drive away ghosts. Place some at the foot of your bed and sleep peacefully.

Chapter 8

Playing with a Long-Gone Boy

When Linda Mackenzie was eight years old, she lived with her parents on Staten Island, New York. It was a tough area where even young children had to be aware of danger on the streets. But Linda was never harmed by anyone. She had an angelic guide that would lead her away from trouble.

A guardian angel

It began one evening when Linda came home from school feeling very tired. She lay down to rest for a while.

When she looked up, she saw the most beautiful white winged figure dressed in pale pink, standing by her bed. There was no sense of fear; Linda felt only peace and joy flooding through her. "This must be an angel," she thought.

In her mind she heard the vision speak, and pictures of places she had never seen appeared; with them came a feeling of pure love. "I will help and lead you," the vision said. From that moment on Linda knew she was protected by a guardian angel.

Often Linda would see a fleeting vision of her angelic guide. The angel would even appear as she walked to or from school or church with her best friend, a girl called Ginger. Sometimes, having seen her protector, a thought would enter her mind: "Don't go that way!" it might say, and she would turn a different corner. Often Linda would learn that she and Ginger had missed some terrible street fight by taking her helper's advice.

To Linda it didn't seem odd that no one else could see her angelic guide; she just accepted it.

Playing with Teddy

One day Linda and Ginger were walking down a street where the houses were old and crumbling. One house had been a fine family home long ago but was now empty and boarded up. Linda and Ginger decided to have a look inside.

The side door was broken and creaked when Linda opened it. As she led the way in, the girls felt as though they had entered another time. Cobwebs hung down from the once grand ceiling and the rooms were dusty and deserted. Yet it felt like a happy place, as though the walls held pleasant memories.

Something caused Linda to turn and look towards a dark corner. There she saw a young boy standing near a spiral staircase. He was wearing strange clothes, but seemed friendly, and he called to Linda to come and look at his room.

Turning to Ginger, Linda said, "Oh, let's go and see!" Without hesitation she ran forward and up the high spiral staircase, following the boy along a hallway to his room.

Inside this room there were many wonderful toys, but they were not modern and there was something not quite right about them that Linda couldn't quite put her finger on. But the boy, who told her his name was Teddy, showed her how to play with them.

Then his mother came in. She was a tall, slim lady wearing an old-fashioned long black dress with a high waist. Linda did not know anyone whose mother dressed like that. But she seemed nice and smiled at Linda.

After a few minutes of playing with young Teddy and his toys, Linda remembered her friend Ginger and said she had to go. After a brief goodbye, she walked back down the winding stairway to where Ginger was standing.

"Oh, I wish you had come with me!" Linda said. "That little boy was so nice!"

For a moment there was silence. "What little boy?"

asked Ginger, looking at her friend as though she were slightly odd.

"Why, the boy who was standing at the bottom of those spiral stairs," Linda replied. She turned to point, but the staircase had completely disappeared. All that remained was a pile of rubble in a corner of the old house. The house was about to be pulled down and the inside of it had already been destroyed.

Afterwards, when Linda questioned Ginger about this incident, she was told that for about twenty minutes her friend had been unable to get her attention. Ginger said that Linda had just stood very still, gazing at the ruins of that old spiral staircase.

The vanishing boy

Some years later Linda and her friend set out to investigate the weird case of the vanishing boy. Looking through books on local history in the library, they found pictures of the house where Linda had seen the spiral staircase and the child who said he was called Teddy. There was even a photograph of a boy with his mother, standing in a room surrounded by toys. This looked like the very room that Linda had visited, and she thought she recognized some of the toys. Underneath the photograph there was a name written: Theodore. Teddy can be short for Theodore.

Life in California

Today Linda Mackenzie lives in Manhattan Beach, California, where she runs a radio show called *Creative Health and Spirit*. She says her life has been one of continuous progression, helped by many angelic guides. Linda believes these guides are messengers from God. A deeply religious person, she teaches that we are all part of a divine plan. Using her now developed psychic and spiritual gifts, Linda has brought hope, healing, and understanding to thousands of people. But she never will forget her ghostly game with a little boy who wasn't there, at the top of a long-gone spiral staircase.

ASSESSMENT

Q: Do you believe that Linda Mackenzie has a guardian angel?

A) If she had one, why would it let her play with ghosts?

B) She is sensitive to dangerous situations and her religion tells her that this is thanks to help from supernatural beings.

C) Something kept Linda and her friend safe from danger. It could very well be Linda's guardian angel.

Chapter 9

Haunted Castles

Great Britain has many ancient castles. These were built hundreds of years ago as strongholds of armies or to house kings, queens, and other members of the nobility. They stand today as monuments to a time long past, when English and Scottish barons and earls ruled their lands by brute force. Dark tales of murder and violence surround many of these old castles. Some say that the ghosts of those who died within those aged walls still walk the night. Here are some of the ghastly ghost stories that live on in the legends of Britain's haunted castles.

The secret horror of Glamis Castle

Glamis Castle stands to the north of Gallow Hill, in the picturesque valley of Strathmore, Tayside, Scotland. This ancient turreted castle holds a secret so terrible that only the Earl of Strathmore and his eldest son and heir are ever told it. The secret is said to concern a hideously deformed child that was born to the family in the early nineteenth century. According to legend, this child grew up and lived to a great age, locked away from sight deep inside the stone walls of Glamis. No one dared look upon the monster because it was so horrible.

Once a worker at the castle chanced to open the secret room where the creature – half man, half beast – was kept prisoner. When he told the Earl what he had seen, the man was given money and persuaded to emigrate. He was thankful to go and he never spoke a word of what he had seen.

Shortly before the thirteenth Earl of Strathmore died in 1904, he told his closest friend about the burden of keeping the dreadful secret of Glamis Castle: "If you

could guess the nature of the secret, you would go down on your knees and thank God it was not yours." He went to his grave without telling anyone except his son and heir. To this very day no one but the Earl of Strathmore knows exactly what kind of monster it was.

The murder of King Malcolm

There are many other legends that have earned Glamis a reputation as Britain's most haunted castle.

The horror began in the year 1034 when Malcolm II of Scotland was hacked to death by a gang of sword-carrying rebels. His blood is said to have soaked into the old oak floor of the room inside Glamis Castle where he died. They say you can still see the bloodstains and, on the anniversary of his murder, hear his ghost screaming in the chill night air.

King Malcolm's killers themselves failed to escape, perishing as they tried to cross a nearby frozen lake, or loch, as they are called in Scotland. The ice cracked as they walked over the loch and the entire gang drowned. Some believe that on a cold winter's night their ghosts still call for help over the frozen waters where they met their end.

The Gray Lady

In the early sixteenth century King James V of Scotland had the Lady of Glamis Castle, Janet Douglas, burned at the stake as a witch. Her ghost is now said to walk the long stone corridors of Glamis. They call her spirit the Gray Lady because she appears as a misty spectre in flowing robes. Slowly she drifts through the lofty halls and dark winding passages within Glamis Castle. Her ghost is thought to be seeking revenge on those who wrongly accused her of witchcraft.

The fate of the Ogilvies

Probably the most horrific story surrounding Glamis concerns the fate of a family that sought refuge there in the fifteenth century. The Ogilvies were feuding with another family, the Lindsays. Seeking safety from their enemy, they arrived at Glamis and begged for protection. It was a deadly mistake, for they would find no friend in this dark castle. The Earl of Strathmore and his men led them deep into the fortified heart of Glamis and locked them all in a strong empty room.

For days and days he never opened the door. The entire family, men, women, and children, were left there to starve. Eventually the rending screams of the Ogilvies caused the Earl to go and see what was happening. When the guards opened the door they saw the most awful sight. The family had turned into cannibals and had begun eating each other.

In absolute horror the Earl bolted the heavy oak and iron door upon them. There the Ogilvies remained until all of them were dead. Their ghosts are now said to scream and moan throughout the castle, making all who hear shudder in terror as they recall the terrible end they met.

The ghost of Balmoral Castle

Deep in the Scottish Grampian Mountains, to the north of Lochnagar, stands the royal castle of Balmoral. Here the Queen and her family come to enjoy the peace and tranquillity of the Highlands. However, there is within the ancient walls of Balmoral Castle a ghost that has, according to reports, been seen by Queen Elizabeth II herself.

Balmoral, like other old castles, has many long winding corridors and halls. Through these walks the ghost of Queen Victoria's personal friend and confidant, her Scottish servant John Brown. He has often been seen in and around the entrance hall, standing tall in his tartan kilt complete with sporran (a fur-covered pouch) and tam-o'shanter (a bobble cap). It has been suggested that they were lovers, so perhaps he is still waiting for the late Queen Victoria.

The ghostly servant of Althorp Park

Diana, Princess of Wales, was brought up in the family mansion of Althorp Park, Northamptonshire, England. This is the stately home of Earl Spencer. It is reported to be haunted by a former servant, whose spirit has been seen by many people.

In 1867 a visiting Church of England clergyman, an archdeacon by the name of Drury, was woken in the middle of the night by a man wearing a striped shirt. Angry at being disturbed, the Archdeacon loudly advised the man to go away and leave him alone. He received no reply from the midnight caller, but the man did turn and walk away into the next room. From that room there was no other exit than the door to the bedroom. When the Archdeacon went to see where the man had gone, he found the room to be empty.

The next day the Archdeacon described the unwanted visitor to his hosts and asked who the man might have been and why he came bothering him in the middle of the night. Lady Lyttleton recognized the description as being that of a house servant. The reason she turned pale was that he had died some weeks before and was now buried in the local graveyard.

Since then the ghostly servant has been seen many times at Althorp Park. Quite recently a visitor to the home of Earl Spencer asked directions of a man he saw standing by a tall tree in the grounds of the stately home. When he spoke to the man, he received no reply. Crossly, the visitor marched off, and when he found another estate worker, he commented on the rude attitude of the man with the striped shirt near the old oak tree. "Why, there's no such person working here," he was told.

But we know that there used to be, over a hundred years ago.

The king's victim

In the year 1541 Catherine Howard married Henry VIII of England to become queen. But young Catherine was not true to her husband the king, and he found out that she had a lover. In a rage Henry ordered Catherine to be taken from their home at Hampton Court Palace to the Tower of London, where she was to be executed.

The palace guards were sent to arrest Queen Catherine in her chambers, while the King knelt in the chapel at Hampton Court saying prayers for her soul. When the captain of the guard arrived, Catherine struggled with the officers who had been sent to drag her off to the Tower. She even managed to escape their grip for a moment and ran down the long gallery of Hampton Court to the door of the chapel, but it was locked. She thumped and banged on the door, yet it remained closed. Inside Henry VIII heard her screaming for mercy, but he hardened his heart. He had cast off his wife and she would die.

On February 15, 1542, Queen Catherine was taken from her cell in the Tower of London to the place of her execution in the courtyard. There she was made to place her head on a block and a black-hooded executioner swung his axe and chopped it off. She is said to have died bravely and never cried.

Since that dreadful day her ghost has been seen many times in Hampton Court Palace. The spirit is often heard running down the long gallery to the chapel. There the ghost of Queen Catherine hammers and bangs on the still locked door. But King Henry VIII is no longer there. He has gone into the history books of old England, along with his lovely young queen, the unfaithful Catherine.

All the above castles are still standing. To the best of the author's knowledge their ghosts remain, unearthly evidence of Britain's haunted heritage.

Chapter 10

The Boy Who Became a Ghost-Hunter

During the 1950s the young Larry Montz was often taken by his mother to visit his aunt Alma and her children. They lived in the French quarter of New Orleans, Louisiana, U.S.A., in a rambling old house that had once been owned by General Pierre Gustave Beauregard.

Beauregard was a general in the Confederate army and the house reflected his status. It was large and had an air of importance about it, as if the building knew it had a proud history. Inside it was crumbling plasterwork, faded curtains, and strangely patterned carpets. The antique furniture was made of heavy oak and leather. But young Larry was happy there; to him that old house felt peaceful. Then one afternoon, when he was just ten years old, he saw a ghost.

A mystery in the attic

Larry used to play with his cousin Michael at Aunt Alma's. Their favorite game was exploring the darkest corners of the old house. It had a great spooky dark basement with cobwebs, and a creaky attic full of stuff from yesteryear. That old house just had to be haunted, Larry thought.

49

One rainy afternoon, as Larry and Michael were coming down the rickety wooden steps from the attic, they saw a strange woman walking in front of them. One minute the hallway before them was empty, the next she was there.

They followed this strange lady into the master bedroom. She had long black hair and was wearing a loose-fitting gray dress. Together Larry and Michael watched as she crossed the room and walked out through the back wall.

Larry was amazed, but he wasn't scared at all. He just wanted to know how something, or someone, could seemingly walk through a solid wall.

First, Larry ran downstairs and told Aunt Alma what the boys had seen. But she told him he was imagining things. "Forget it!" she said. "It must have been a hallucination."

Later, back at his own home, Larry told his mother about the ghostly woman. She laughed out loud and said it was the silliest story she had heard that week.

But ten-year-old Larry was certain that he hadn't just been seeing things. He was convinced that he could trust the evidence of his senses. What did puzzle him was the how and why of the phenomenon. Why had the ghost appeared? And how did it walk through solid matter? Larry was determined to find out.

The start of an unusual career

Larry Montz gave up on repeating his story to adults. They thought he was either joking or nuts. So from then on, every time he visited Aunt Alma's house, he kept a written record of what he saw, but he said nothing.

Time after time Larry and his cousin Michael saw the ghostly woman walk into that old bedroom and exit through the wall that faced the rear garden. When he looked out the window after her, Larry saw only an old

oak tree and moss-covered stone paths, almost hidden among the overgrown flowerbeds. The lady in gray was nowhere to be seen. She had vanished as if into thin air.

As the years passed, Larry became too involved in his studies to spend much time on ghost-watching. His visits to Aunt Alma's grew fewer and further between.

At university, Larry studied electrical engineering. But this practical subject did not fully occupy his mind. Larry could not forget his ghostly encounter with the lady in gray.

When he had completed his engineering degree, Larry decided to switch to another field, one that covered his special interest. There is a branch of psychology called parapsychology. This is the scientific study of unexplained phenomena like thought transference and ghost sightings.

After more years of study, Larry Montz obtained a doctorate in parapsychology. Now he could begin to do what he had dreamed of doing ever since he was a ten-year-old boy. He was going to discover the how and the why of such things as ghosts.

Ghost-hunters' research institute

In 1972 Larry Montz formed the International Society for Paranormal Research. He gathered around him a team of scientists and set about investigating hauntings, ghosts, and all things supernatural. He had become a real-life ghostbuster.

Today the International Society for Paranormal Research involves scientists, parapsychologists, and mediums worldwide. They are all working together to prove the truth, or otherwise, of supernatural happenings. Their headquarters are in Los Angeles, in the haunted Vogue Theatre, Hollywood. From there Dr. Montz and his team organize ghost-hunting expeditions around the world.

When asked whether he still believed in ghosts, Dr. Montz said, "The scientific evidence that we at the ISPR have gathered proves that ghosts are a reality. They do exist, but at a different level of vibration from 'living' physical human beings. They can sometimes be seen and I have seen many. My first was a long time ago, in the French quarter of New Orleans, when I was just a boy."

ASSESSMENT

Q: Why do you think young Larry Montz's mother and aunt told him he was being silly when he reported seeing a ghost?

A) Because he was mistaken. Ghosts are hallucinations.

B) They did not want Larry to be scared.

C) Adults are like that, they don't want to believe in ghosts or haunted houses at all. Adults only accept scientific facts.

Chapter 11

Scientific Secrets of Ghost-Hunting Expeditions

The International Society for Paranormal Research is still headed by its founder, Larry Montz. This dedicated and learned professional leads a team that includes both technical and scientific experts and highly sensitive individuals with para-normal powers. Dr. Montz believes that it is the combination of psychic mediums and scientists working together that helps the ISPR to gain the best results.

Dr. Montz has brought in the latest scientific devices to test for physical signs of ghosts in houses and other areas where his team of psychic mediums locate them. This chapter describes some of the technical equipment used by the ISPR in their investigations.

Electronic temperature gauges

A spirit or ghostly presence is said to create a cold spot in the area that is occupied by its usually invisible body. The difference in temperature can be as much as 15-20 degrees Fahrenheit (up to 10 degrees Celsius). To locate such cold spots, the ISPR investigators use electronic

temperature gauges that are easy to read and highly accurate. These temperature differences are recorded by the ISPR team on a map of the place that is said to be haunted.

Electronic magnetometers

A given area will have its own constant electromagnetic field. This can be measured by a magnetometer. A ghost has an electromagnetic field which is different from that of the area it haunts. The ISPR investigators search the site of a reported haunting with a magnetometer, looking for changes in the electromagnetic field. Where the electromagnetic field varies, they suspect a ghost, and any movement of such a field is taken to indicate the movement of the ghost. All electromagnetic changes are recorded on the site map.

Motion-detectors

A motion-detector works by sending out constant infrared beams. If anything moves within the area covered by these beams, an alarm, a light, or a camera is triggered. Such devices are to be found outside many homes as security aids to deter burglars.

The ISPR investigators use specially designed motion-detectors to locate the unseen movements of spirit beings. They place them in the spots where a ghost is most likely to be found, according to their other equipment or the psychic medium.

Infrared video

Scientists originally developed night-vision

rifle sights, binoculars, and cameras for use by the armed forces. These enable users to see in almost total darkness through the infrared light spectrum. They register cold as blue or purple and heat as bright orange or red.

The ISPR investigators use video cameras adapted for infrared vision. They set up these video cameras in areas where ghosts have been reported. Often they are linked electronically to motion-detectors so that any movement by spirits in the dark is automatically recorded on these cameras.

The ISPR investigators may also set up a TV monitor which displays the temperature images seen by this camera. When the lack of heat in a specific area shows in a blue or purple, almost human shape, this is taken to be a ghost.

High-speed and Polaroid films

There is no special film for photographing ghosts. However, standard high-speed 35-mm film is better at recording in low light than ordinary film. This film can capture streaks of light or slightly luminous mists, which are often thought to be the visible image of a spirit being. Sometimes, if the ISPR team are lucky, they may capture the outline of a ghost.

Polaroid instant cameras are ideal for very quick results and are often used by ISPR investigators to provide evidence of a spirit presence during an investigation. Still cameras are often linked to motion-detectors.

Audio-tape recorders

The ISPR teams use standard audio-cassette or reel-to-reel tape recorders with an open microphone. The team may use more than one tape recorder on an investigation, depending on the requirements of the site. Professional-quality audio tape is best, for there can be a slight hum with standard tapes. The microphone is placed in a strategic position and the tape recorder is switched on to record. Some machines have sound-sensitive devices that automatically start the recording process when they register a noise.

Take part in a real ghost-hunting expedition!

Some of the ISPR's ghost-hunting expeditions are open to the general public. These offer a visit to a haunted house that has been fully investigated and determined to be "active." Participants are invited to search and – who knows? – may experience ghost contact. They are shown by qualified ISPR investigators how to use some of the above-mentioned equipment. There will also be an opportunity for expedition members to test their own psychic ability under the guidance of an ISPR medium.

For details you can contact the ISPR via the Internet at www.hauntings.com or at www.ispr.net.

A ghostly mist in front of a haunted house.

Dr. Larry Montz leading a team of ISPR investigators inside the haunted Vogue Theatre, Hollywood, L.A.

Chapter 12

How to Conduct Your Own Spook Hunt

Simply follow the steps on the check-chart below. Remember: always work as a team of at least three people and make sure that one of your team is an adult. Spook-hunting is fun, but it can be scary too.

The adult is the team leader and therefore No. 1. The person with the highest score in the Personal Spook-Sensitivity Test (below) is No. 2, the psychic investigator. No. 3 is the technical investigator, using the equipment.

There can be more than one technical investigator, depending on the size of your team and the equipment used. At the very least, each team member should have a pen and a pad of plain paper to record observations.

Spook-hunting team members

No. 1: ADULT

Name_____ Age____

Address_____

_____

Zip Code_____ Tel. _____

No. 2: PSYCHIC INVESTIGATOR

Name_____ Age____

Address_____

_____

Zip Code_____ Tel. _____

No. 3: TECHNICAL INVESTIGATOR

Name_____ Age____

Address_____

_____

Zip Code_____ Tel. _____

Team duties

No. 1, team leader

a) Maintain control of the team.
b) Before the start of the spook hunt, assess the possibility that the area to be covered is haunted.
c) Draw a map of the site or area.
d) Mark on the map all points where spooks have been reported.
e) Supervise the psychic search of your No. 2, noting his/her observations.
f) Decide on the plan for action and set a firm date and time.
g) Organize equipment and allocate it to the team members.
h) Ensure your team members know how to use the equipment.
i) Lead your team on the spook hunt.

j) Keep full records with names of all team members and copies of films, photographs, temperature charts, tape recordings, etc.

k) Make a fully documented report.

l) Call your team together and discuss the results of the spook hunt.

No. 2, psychic investigator

a) Conduct a psychic search of the area or site. Don't go anywhere you're not allowed!

b) Report to No. 1 any place that you feel has a spooky presence or sense of a ghost about it.

c) Even if you see a spook, remain calm and always obey the instructions of your team leader.

d) Your place is with the team leader unless you are sent elsewhere.

e) Keep your psychic senses alert! You may be the key to the success of the hunt.

f) Make certain you know the signal to abandon the spook hunt.

No. 3, technical investigator

a) Following the instructions of No. 1, use your equipment to its best advantage.

b) Make sure you know how your equipment works.

c) Keep very detailed records of everything you see or hear.

d) Report anything that might be a spook to your team leader.

e) Be aware at all times of the whereabouts of No. 1 and/or your nearest team member.

f) Never question the decisions of the team leader.
g) Make certain you know the signal to abandon the spook hunt.

Step-by-step spook-hunting

1) Team leader to interview all those who report sightings of ghosts or spooky happenings. These statements should be written down and kept on file. If possible, get those interviewed to sign and date them, giving their full name and address with a contact telephone number.

2) Draw a detailed map of the site involved.

3) On the map, mark the areas where spooky stuff has been reported. For example:

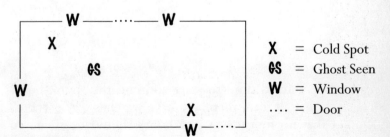

X = Cold Spot
GS = Ghost Seen
W = Window
.... = Door

4) No. 2, the psychic investigator, should search the area. Mark findings on the map as in the example on page 61.

5) Team leader should have equipment ready. Prepare your team for action on a specific time and date, as agreed with the owners of the supposedly haunted house.

6) On the day/night of the spook hunt, count all your team and agree a signal to abandon the building if things get too spooky.

7) Position your No. 3 and any other technical investigators with their equipment in the places indicated by No. 2. Make sure that you leave no team member alone.

8) Agree a fixed time to start and end the spook hunt. (Check that all team members have watches!) We recommend that no more than two hours should be spent on each spook hunt. No. 1 is responsible for checking all team members in and out of the site of the spook hunt.

Use a check list if there are many of you.

Remember to make sure all the team members' parents or guardians know exactly where you are going and what you are doing.

9) During the time the spook hunt is taking place, strict silence should be maintained. All team members should concentrate on observing and recording all spooky phenomena.

10) After the spook hunt, the team leader takes all notes, films, tapes, temperature measurements, etc., and writes a detailed report based on these.

CAUTION!

YOU MUST NOT ATTEMPT THIS WITHOUT PERMISSION FROM YOUR PARENT OR GUARDIAN. AN ADULT OF 21 OR OLDER SHOULD ACT AS THE TEAM LEADER.

Chapter 13

Personal Spook-Sensitivity Test

This test is designed to determine your potential to see ghosts and phantoms. Simply place a tick alongside the statements to which you can answer YES. Then total all your YES answers and refer to the assessment to see for yourself whether you have the psychic potential to be a spook-hunter.

1) Have you ever seen what you believed to be a ghost?

2) Do you recall your dreams clearly?

3) Do you ever find money or treats by your bedside that no one admits to having placed there?

4) When entering a house or a castle for the first time, have you ever felt a heavy or uncomfortable atmosphere?

5) Have you ever misplaced something and later found it in a place where you're sure you didn't lose it?

6) Do you ever have a feeling that some stranger or place is evil?

7) In any of your dreams, have you experienced something that later actually happened?

8) In a strange house, have you ever found an inexplicably cold spot?

9) Have you ever smelled the scent of perfume or flowers with no visible source?

10) As a young child, did you ever see visions of distant lands playing before your eyes when you gazed at a blank wall?

11) Have you ever seen mysterious bright lights floating through a room?

12) Have you ever visited a strange town and thought you had been there before?

13) Have you ever turned quickly, thinking someone was behind you, only to discover that you were alone?

14) Have you ever had a feeling that something was about to happen, then it did?

15) As a young child, did you have a friend that was invisible to everyone else?

16) Do you find that electrical equipment fails to work or works in a strange way when you are near it?

17) Have you ever met a total stranger that you thought you had met before?

18) Have you ever picked up an object, say an old watch, and had impressions of the person or persons that previously owned it?

19) During the night, have you ever woken to see a strange white mist in your room?

20) Have you ever heard a voice call your name when no one was there?

Your spook-sensitivity assessment

Total **YES** answers:

15 upwards: You are able to see ghosts, if you want to.

10-14: You will be a great help on any spook hunt.

5-9: You have some sensitivity to spooky phenomena. Join the hunt!

0-4: Every spook hunt can use a person who won't get scared, and that's you.

Chapter 17

The Ghost Cat

Maria Woods of Southport, Lancashire, England, was just seven years old when she met her first ghost. This was no spooky white misty shape, but a creature that looked perfectly real. Yet it was a

messenger from the next world, a ghost cat which appeared to the young Maria as an omen of death.

The girl, the cat, and the wardrobe

It was a chilly afternoon one Sunday in late October and Maria was bored. She had read all her comics twice and was fed up with coloring pictures in. As she sat at the old oak table, absentmindedly drawing a beard on a lady in some TV magazine, Maria glimpsed something moving out of the corner of her eye. Looking up, she saw a large brown and white cat walking out of the door towards the stairs in the hallway. Thinking this was very odd, as the family did not own a cat, Maria jumped off her chair and followed the creature.

Up the stairs went the cat, never looking back, just climbing the steps one at a time. At the top the cat turned right on the landing and walked into Maria's bedroom. She followed close behind, curious to see where this strange cat might be going. Inside her room Maria watched in wonder as the fat cat pushed open her wooden wardrobe door and crawled inside. When Maria opened it wider to see what the cat was doing, she was astounded. The cat had vanished.

One white ear and one brown

That evening as Maria sat with her mother eating dinner, she was told to be a brave girl because there was some sad news. That afternoon Mrs. Taylor, a family friend, had died. Maria had known this nice, kindly lady all her life and was very sorry to learn of her death. But she did not link it to the mysterious cat.

Some weeks later, Maria stood in the bathroom cleaning her teeth before school. Suddenly, out of the corner of her eye, she saw the cat. It was the same one as before, brown and white. Dropping her toothbrush in the sink, Maria quickly left the bathroom and followed the mystery cat. As before, it walked into her bedroom, pushed open the wardrobe door with its paw and crawled in.

Instantly Maria threw the wardrobe door wide open and stared inside. No cat was to be seen. Once again the creature had vanished into thin air.

That night Maria was watching TV when the telephone rang. Her mother went to answer it and came back in tears. "What's the matter, Mum?" Maria asked, putting her arm around her mother's shoulder.

"My aunt Mary died this morning at eight," she said between sobs.

That's when Maria thought about the cat. It was around eight in the morning that she had seen the strange creature. But she did not ask her mother about it until a few days later.

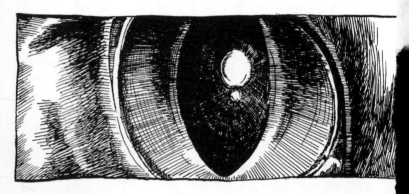

"Mummy, do you know there's a cat in the house sometimes?"

Her mother replied that she was certain no cat ever came in. The doors and windows were usually closed. Then Maria told her mother how she had seen the strange cat and explained that it always disappeared in her wardrobe. Her mother looked incredulous. Then Maria described the cat.

"Why, that sounds just like my pussycat Timmy that I owned when I was a girl about your age!" her mother said. "Did it have one white ear and one brown?"

Maria told her that it did.

For a moment there was total silence in the house.

"You must tell me at once the next time you see that cat," Maria's mother said. "I think it might be a ghost."

Young Maria was a little scared, and she promised to tell her mother as soon as she saw the cat again.

Another death

Months passed and Maria had all but forgotten about the cat. Then, one evening in February, she saw it again. Maria was just getting ready for bed when in walked the ghost cat and climbed into the wardrobe. This time Maria ran for her mother.

"Mummy, Mummy!" she called. "Quick! The cat's just gone into my wardrobe."

Maria's mother ran up the stairs and into the bedroom. Flinging open the door of the old pine wardrobe, she peered inside. There in the darkness on the floor of the wardrobe was a pair of shoes and a crumpled school dress. But no cat.

Maria went to bed, but she could not sleep. The fear of seeing that ghostly cat kept her awake. Just before midnight she heard a thumping and banging on the front door of the house. Her mother went reluctantly downstairs to see who was calling at this time of night. It turned out to be her friend Barry who lived next door. "What's wrong?" she asked, wondering why her neighbor was out in the witching hour.

In her bedroom Maria listened in terror to the reply. "It's my wife," he said. "She died this evening."

As Maria looked in the darkness towards the half-open door of her wardrobe, she saw something green and twinkling in the moonlight. Something that looked just like the emerald eyes of a cat.

Never again!

Over the years Maria saw the ghost cat many times. Each time someone known to her family died. For some reason the sightings stopped when she became a young woman. Today Maria Woods is certain that the spirit of her mother's childhood cat Timmy was returning to warn the family of a forthcoming death.

When I spoke to Maria in her home, she told me she now owns three pet cats and they bring her a lot of comfort and joy. But one thing she dreads is seeing the terrifying ghost cat ever again. And each night she makes certain that her wardrobe door is firmly shut. Who can blame her?

ASSESSMENT

Q: Do you think a ghost cat would come to warn Maria of a forthcoming death?

A) I don't think there ever was a ghost cat. Just a bored little girl who got fed up drawing beards on ladies' pictures.

B) It may be that Maria is psychic and her mind invents the symbol of a cat as a warning to her.

C) I think the cat is the ghost of Maria's mother's cat, and it can see the future. As it is Maria's friend, it visits from the next world to tell her of the tragedy to come.

The Man in Black

At sixteen, Audrey Angelo was really too old to jump into her parents' bed because she was scared. But a monster movie she had just seen had frightened her so much that she could not sleep. In the shadowy corners of her darkened room she seemed to see something moving – something unnatural and horrible.

Staying there alone with the invisible menace eventually seemed worse to her than being thought a baby, and she fled to her parents' bedroom.

Finally falling asleep next to her mother, Audrey had a bad dream. In this dream she could see a tall, thin man, slightly stooped, wearing a black three-piece suit, so dark that it seemed to

71

shimmer. The jacket was unfashionably long and from his waistcoat pocket there hung a gold watch on the end of a chain. When she looked into the man's eyes, Audrey saw only shadows.

He's back!

With a scream Audrey woke up and grabbed her mother's arm. "There's a man in black!" she cried, trembling.

At her side Mrs. Annie Angelo was instantly awake. "Tell me what you saw, Audrey," she said, comforting her just as she had done when her daughter was a child.

"He wears all black!" Audrey whimpered, unable to explain why this figure terrified her so.

Audrey's mother turned to Mr. Angelo on the far side of the bed. "Did you hear that, Albert?" she said.

To her amazement, Audrey heard her father reply, "He's back!"

Mrs. Angelo turned the lights on and got out of bed. Leaving her husband to go back to sleep, she took Audrey to the kitchen to make her a cup of hot chocolate. As the friendly lamplight and the sweet drink restored a feeling of normality to the night, Mrs. Angelo explained what Audrey's father had meant by that ominous remark, "He's back!"

Many years ago, when Audrey was only two or three years old, she would often waken the house with her cries. When asked what the matter was she could only say that she had dreamed of a man in black. The dreams had stopped when the family moved house from Westminster to Fullerton, where they now lived – both places are in the greater Los Angeles area of California. But now, it seemed, the man in black had caught up with her.

No one in the family had a clue who this man in black might be. But the more often Audrey dreamed of him, the scarier he seemed.

Grandmother says goodbye

Two years passed before the mystery of the man in black was solved. Audrey and her parents had moved to Frankfurt in Germany, where Mr. Angelo was working on an engineering contract. Hearing that his mother was seriously ill, he flew the family back to California to try to see her in hospital. But just a few hours before they arrived, the old lady died.

Audrey was crying. She had loved her grandmother and now she would never see her again. Her father was equally sad. He had tried so hard to get everyone back in time to tell his mother they loved her before she passed away. Now she was gone and they had not even said goodbye.

That night they stayed in a hotel in Anaheim. It was full and Audrey, now eighteen, had to share a room with her parents. It took a while for her to fall asleep, and when she did, the dream of the man in black returned.

It woke her at once, but this time she was not frightened. There was a strange feeling of peace in the room. Audrey opened her eyes and in the darkness she saw a silvery gray mist floating at the foot of the bed.

Her father was also awake and heard Audrey gasp. "Don't be afraid," he said. "Grandma just wants to say goodbye."

Audrey saw a shape form within the mist. It was her beloved grandmother. She was there and smiling so peacefully that Audrey almost cried out in joy.

Turning to her father, she saw that he was crying tears of happiness. As he dried his eyes, Albert Angelo said, "Sleep now, Audrey! We have said goodbye." At once she was deeply asleep.

Was he real?

The next morning the family were taken to the funeral

parlor in nearby Norwalk to pay their respects to the grandmother they had loved. Audrey led the way up to the entrance, a heavy oak door with an old brass bell. She rang it and waited.

As the door inched open, she began to tremble. There before her stood the man in black. He was tall, slightly stooped and very thin. His jacket was long and so dark that it almost shimmered. From his waistcoat pocket hung a gold watch on a chain, and his eyes were like dark shadows.

He was the undertaker at the funeral parlor. But Audrey knew that wherever her grandmother had gone, she was beyond his reach.

ASSESSMENT

Q: Why do you think Audrey had dreams of the man in black?

A) Such figures often feature in scary films. Audrey and her parents then identified it with her earlier nightmares, which none of them could really remember in any detail.

B) Perhaps Audrey had been frightened by the sight of an undertaker when she was very little.

C) In the dream, the man in black was given to Audrey as an omen of death.

Is Your Family Haunted?

Test your family and friends

Have you ever wondered if there is a family ghost? Who knows, someone in your family may have seen a ghost or had a sense of something supernatural going on. Here's what to ask your grandparents or that odd uncle of yours. You may be surprised at the stories they can tell. Just ask them these ten simple questions and tick YES or NO, then refer to the assessment chart to see if your family is haunted. Try the test on your friends as well!

1) Have you ever been very frightened by something strange in the dark? YES ___ NO ___
2) Have you ever seen anything you thought might be a ghost? YES ___ NO ___
3) Are there any stories in our family of people seeing ghosts? YES ___ NO ___
4) Have you ever heard weird noises in the night that you could not explain? YES ___ NO ___
5) Is there a legend within the family of some spooky omen of death, like the appearance of a black bird or the sound of wailing? YES ___ NO ___

6) Have you ever seen a headless horse or other phantom animal?   YES ___ NO ___

7) Have you ever felt yourself inexplicably transported back in time?   YES ___ NO ___

8) Have you ever levitated or floated about the room unsupported?   YES ___ NO ___

9) Have you ever looked in the mirror and seen a face you did not recognize?   YES ___ NO ___

10) Have you ever felt ghostly hands touching you in the night?   YES ___ NO ___

8-10 YES answers Your family name isn't Addams, by any chance?

5-7 YES answers Your family is very haunted and spooky indeed. Look out when the moon is full, whooo!

3-4 YES answers There is certainly something pretty weird about you lot. Better buy some garlic!

1-2 YES answers You may have a small ghost, or just a nervous auntie. Read on before you decide.

0 YES answers No ghosts, no spooks – never mind! Try the neighbors, they look very weird.

NOTE

You might like to use a cassette recorder to tape any spooky stories your family members may tell you. Then you will have a record of all the details.

Sassy: A Dog That Sees Ghosts

Sassy is the family pet of the Nailon family in Cape May, New Jersey, U.S.A. They think she can see ghosts, and so can others in the house.

Phantom fuzz balls

It all began in 1994 when the family first moved into their new home. One night young Shaun, aged four at the time, said he kept hearing someone who wasn't there, calling his name. His younger sister Kaitlyn, then three years old, told her mother that the house had lots of "fuzz balls" floating in the air.

No one else could see any fuzz balls, and Cathy Nailon at first thought that her children were imagining these weird things. But one evening she too got spooked.

The voice in the night

It was almost 1 a.m., and Cathy was at her personal computer logged on to the Internet. Her husband Robert had gone to bed and both the children were fast asleep. Sassy, the dog, was sitting quietly at Cathy's feet, keeping her company as she sent messages to her Internet buddies around the world.

Suddenly Sassy jumped up and bared her teeth, growling fiercely. Cathy looked around, but there was no one to be seen. Then she heard a voice calling, "Catherine, are you coming to bed?"

"Just a minute," she replied, thinking it was Robert. "I'll log off and close the PC down."

Sassy remained standing as Cathy began shutting down her computer. The dog seemed very scared, as if there was a burglar or something nasty around. Then Cathy heard the voice again: "Catherine! When are you coming to bed?"

This time Sassy went crazy, howling and barking at what looked to Cathy like thin air. She stroked and tried to comfort her pet but the dog remained very uneasy.

Cathy thought it strange that Robert kept calling her — he had never done that before. She went to ask him why he was shouting and disturbing the dog.

Entering the bedroom, Cathy said, "Why are you calling me? You don't usually ..."

Robert said nothing. He was fast asleep.

Wondering if he was just pretending, Cathy shook her husband's shoulder and again asked why he had been shouting. He yawned, opened his eyes, and replied that he hadn't said anything. Then he turned over and went straight back to sleep.

The next morning Cathy questioned her husband about the voice in the middle of the night, but he knew nothing about it. Robert had been in the land of dreams.

An unseen someone

Since that day Sassy the dog has been behaving very strangely. She often walks into empty rooms and growls for no reason that Cathy can see. Sassy's eyes seem to be following something that, to Cathy, is invisible. Kaitlyn, who is now six years old, still says that the house is full of white fuzzy balls that float about, and Shaun reports that an unseen someone continues to shout his name.

The Nailon family are sure their home is haunted, but by whom? Only Sassy seems to know, and she's saying nothing but "Grrrrrr!"

ASSESSMENT

 Q: Do you think that something is haunting the Nailons' house?

A) Of course not. The husband talks in his sleep, the dog is nervous, and the children are too small to know what they're saying.

B) Sassy is growling at dandelion fluff – that is the fuzzy white stuff floating around the house.

C) Dogs are known to be sensitive to spirits and Sassy must be seeing the ghost that the Nailon family cannot see.

A Door into the Past

Lesley Shepherd was 12 years old when she crossed over an invisible barrier and stepped into a world long gone.

Did she see ghosts, or was she herself the ghost?

A visit to Bent Brook Farm

The high school was planning a fund-raising sale and all the children were asked to collect unwanted goods and gifts from around their area. Lesley lived in a semi-rural district some miles from the school. Her parents ran a little farm and all the neighbors were cattle or pig farmers. Taking the preprinted sheets advertising the event, which the teacher had given her, Lesley set off first thing Saturday morning round the local farmhouses. It was a long walk up to each house because they were set within acres and acres of land.

Just before noon Lesley arrived at the winding dirt track leading to Bent Brook Farm, the final call on her list. She knew one of the children who lived there, Colin Grainey, and hoped for a good response. She and Colin had been friends from early childhood, though he went to a different school in another part of the district.

As she walked along the hawthorn-edged path, Lesley realized how tired she was. This Saturday was the last in June and the summer sun beat down on the dusty track.

A blackbird sang its solitary song. Looking across the fields, Lesley could see the bird sitting on the uppermost branch of an old, twisted tree. "Thank goodness this is the last place!" she thought as, turning a final corner, she saw the house of Bent Brook Farm.

She knocked on the big oak and iron door, but no one came. She knocked again. "Oh, please let them be home!" she said to herself. She did not want to have to return the next day.

Still there was nothing but silence and summer sunshine. Then Lesley saw that the front door was ever so slightly open. She pushed it a little, and the old door creaked as it inched wider.

"Is there anybody there?" she called out in a rather small voice.

Listening carefully, Lesley heard nothing but the buzzing of insects and the song of that now faraway blackbird. Thinking to leave her piece of paper on the hall table, she stepped through the heavy old door into the dark house.

It was cold inside, and a shiver ran through her.

The place felt as if the sun never shone there. As she reached forward to place her sheet of paper on a table near the front door, Lesley saw someone. It was a lady, a very old lady, who sat gently rocking backward and forward in her chair. She was wearing a blue-patterned dress; her silver hair was tied back and one long curl hung over her shoulder.

Lesley's eyes got used to the gloom and she saw two little children playing at the old lady's feet. They were moving building bricks around to make shapes, and seemed unaware that Lesley was there.

"I've come to deliver this note from my school," Lesley said.

At this point the old woman noticed her. She smiled and pointed to the mantelpiece. "Leave it there, my dear," she said in voice that mysteriously echoed around the room.

In the fireplace there was a log fire burning, despite the heat of the summer day outside.

"It's our playtime," the old lady said, looking down at the two children sitting on the bare, stone-flagged floor.

Placing her sheet of paper on the mantelpiece, Lesley turned to leave. "Thank you," she said, but the old lady made no reply. Rocking gently, she seemed almost asleep.

Lesley took one last look at the two children. They were strangely dressed in what looked like home-made clothes. The older child, a boy of about five, had curly blond hair, and the younger, a girl, had long black hair. Both ignored Lesley as though she were not there.

The wrong farm?

The next week the schoolteacher said it was time to go back around the houses where the printed requests for goods had been delivered by the children. This time Lesley thought she would start at Bent Brook Farm and work her way back from there.

Once again it was a hot day and the dirt track leading to the old house was even dustier. As Lesley walked up to the front of the farmhouse, she noticed something very odd. The oak and iron door was not there! Instead there was a new blue-painted door with a big brass knocker and a pinewood sign that read "Bent Brook Farm." Outside the house was Mr. Grainey, repairing a tractor with his son Colin.

"Hello, Mr. Grainey," Lesley said. "I've come to collect anything you want to give to our school sale."

Mr. Grainey shook his head. "Don't know anything about it," he replied.

Lesley told him that she had delivered a note from her teacher just the week before, and the old lady had said to leave it on the mantelpiece. He still looked puzzled, so Lesley described the children.

"Why, there's no old lady here," said Mr. Grainey, "and certainly no little children."

When Lesley insisted that there had been, he took her into the farmhouse and asked her to show him where she had seen all this. But she couldn't.

The entire room had changed. The stone-flagged floor was now carpeted, and where the old lady's rocking chair had stood was a TV set. Even the fireplace had been altered completely and instead of an open grate with burning logs, there was a modern gas fire.

At first Lesley thought she might have imagined this, or taken a wrong turning and gone to another farm. But as she walked slowly back down the dusty track leading from Bent Brook Farm, she heard a blackbird singing in the near distance. Looking out across the green fields, she saw a twisted old oak tree. There on the top branch was the bird singing his solitary song, just as he had been the week before.

A door in time

To this very day Lesley is certain that she saw old Bent Brook Farm as it had been perhaps a century before. On that summer's day the door between the past and the present had parted to let Lesley in. She still wonders what might had have happened if that door had closed behind her. Perhaps she would never have been seen in this world again!

ASSESSMENT

Q: Did Lesley really walk into another world and see Bent Brook Farm as it was many years ago?

A) Lesley was so hot and tired from her long walk that she saw a hallucination.

B) Lesley may have fallen asleep in the sun and dreamed about the old lady and the two children.

C) Yes, she did see into another world, one that exists in the distant past.

Chapter 19

Screaming Skulls

The legends of screaming skulls are among the most frightening in the mysterious world of ghosts. Since time began, our ancestors all over the world have believed that it is important that the physical remains of a dead person be treated with respect. But some bodies are not allowed to rest in peace. Some are cut in pieces and have their heads removed. Others are not buried in a place where they can rest, and so their spirits are said to return. These are the ghosts that haunt their own mortal remains, and they are called screaming skulls.

The screaming skull of Slaithwaite

There are few more solemn experiences than staring into the empty sockets of a human skull. Imagine how much more frightening this is when you believe that you are looking at a real screaming skull. In my research I had to brave the horror of meeting face to bone the screaming skull of Slaithwaite

In the eighteenth century, members of the medical profession were finding out how the human body is put together and what the different organs do. To this end doctors and surgeons needed dead bodies to examine. This would involve cutting into the corpse and removing vital organs such as the heart, liver, and lungs. There were religious objections to this because of a literal belief in the resurrection of the dead. But doctors and students received the bodies of hanged criminals, and in addition they bought corpses that had been dug up secretly from graveyards. The people who engaged in this grisly trade were known as body-snatchers or resurrection men.

Slaithwaite is a small village in Yorkshire, England, on the outskirts of Huddersfield. In the early eighteenth century the industry would have been the weaving of cotton fabric, with the local weavers working at handlooms in their cottages. In keeping with tradition, the families buried their dead in the churchyard. It was from there that a gang of body snatchers stole a fresh corpse and sold it to a surgeon for experiments. When the experiments were over, the skull was used as an exhibit for medical students to examine. That was until it began to scream.

According to local legend, on the anniversary of its removal from the Slaithwaite churchyard, the skull screamed. All who heard it were horrified.

Today the screaming skull of Slaithwaite tours the United Kingdom in a museum exhibition. I met this scary skull in the Harris Museum, Preston, Lancashire. The curator agreed to let me hold it and look at it close up to see if it might scream for me. But of course I don't know which day is its screaming day.

As I stared deep into the dark, empty sockets, I felt cold inside. Then I swear I saw the jawbone move. But I heard no scream, only the thud-thud-thud of my terrified heart.

The screaming skull of the martyred priest

Wardley Hall in Lancashire, England, has within it the skull of a Roman Catholic priest, Father Ambrose Barlow. This priest was executed in the year 1640 during a period of religious persecution. His head was hacked from his body and stuck up on a spike. This was meant as a warning to all who thought to follow the teachings of the priest or his church.

But not everyone was frightened of the killers of Father Barlow. The owners of Wardley Hall rescued the priest's head and placed it in a hidden case at the top of the hall's main staircase. There it remained quietly for almost three hundred years.

Then, in 1930, some thieves broke into Wardley Hall and stole many valuable things. They also took the skull of Father Barlow. This was a serious mistake that they soon regretted.

According to legend, as the thieves sat checking their booty, the skull of Father Ambrose Barlow let out a terrifying scream. In horror the thieves ran from their den and never returned.

The skull was later discovered and taken back to Wardley Hall. There a local Catholic priest tried to give it a Christian burial in the church graveyard.

That night Wardley Hall was hit by a powerful thunderstorm, which seemed to be directly above the old house. As the lightning flashed and the wind rattled the doors of the ancient building, a terrible muffled scream was heard coming from the graveyard. It was the screaming skull of the long-dead Father Barlow.

The screaming skull was later returned to its original resting place in a glass case at the top of Wardley Hall's old staircase. There it remains to this very day, silently resting, at least for the time being.

The screaming skull of Bettiscombe

In the middle of the eighteenth century the Pinney family of Bettiscombe village in Devon, southwest England, had a servant from the African continent working for them. This man was a good, honest person who dedicated his days to working for the household. He served the Pinney family for many years and his only request was that before he died he would be sent home to Africa, so that he could be buried in his homeland. The head of the family, John Frederick Pinney, promised him this in return for all his long years of good service.

Eventually the servant was taken ill and he knew he was dying. On his deathbed he pleaded with John F. Pinney to return his body to Africa for burial. This was promised to him and the man died in peace.

However, the promise was broken. Instead of shipping their servant's body back to Africa, the Pinney family had it buried in the local graveyard. It did not remain buried for very long.

Shortly after the funeral, the entire village of Bettiscombe was rocked by violent thunderstorms. Horrible shrieks could be heard echoing through the night, and all who lived in the tiny village were terrified. The screams were traced to the graveyard, where they seemed to be coming from beneath the ground, just where the African servant lay.

The next day the Pinney family dug up the dead man's body and returned it to their manor house, where it was stored under the roof. The screaming and disturbances then stopped.

Years later another member of the Pinney family tried to bury the skeleton of the long-dead servant in the garden of the house. Three days later the skull was discovered at the side of its burial mound. People said it had dug its way out of the grave with its teeth.

That night frightful screams were heard and again the thunder crashed and lightning flashed over that old village. In terror the Pinney family returned the screaming skull to the house and placed it inside the brickwork, where it was walled in. To this day no one dares to disturb it for fear the skull may scream again.

Some believe the ghost of the dead servant will never rest until his skeleton is returned to Africa. But that can never be, for only his screaming skull remains. The rest of his bones are forever lost in the haunted village of Bettiscombe.

A Classroom on the Other Side

Kathy Stuart was just a child of four when the nightmares began. Her natural mother and father had been unable to care for their child and at the age of two Kathy had been adopted by a caring couple in the town of Belfast, Maine, U.S.A. But, despite all the love they gave her, Kathy suffered from vivid dreams that led to sleepwalking in this world and, Kathy believes, the next.

Often Kathy would wake to find herself out of her bed and in another part of the house. These night-time wanderings worried the middle-aged couple who had adopted her. Mr. and Mrs. Stuart had already brought up their own daughter, Jeanne. She was now married and lived with her husband Eddis and their little son Geoffrey in Boston, Massachusetts. But the Stuarts had never seen Jeanne, or any other child, sleepwalking.

There seemed no reason for Kathy to suffer from bad dreams. She was well cared for – spoiled, she says now. When asked why she took her almost nightly walks from bed, Kathy spoke of mysterious meetings with people who simply were not there. Mr. and Mrs. Stuart listened carefully, but thought only that she had been dreaming or was inventing her strange stories. They took her to a doctor, who said she might be suffering from stomach trouble brought on by eating too late in the evening. But changing

her diet and her mealtimes did nothing to stop Kathy
from walking in her sleep.

A lesson about the afterlife

One late October evening in 1959, just before Kathy's
fifth birthday, she awoke – as she thought – to find herself
not in another part of her home, but in a setting she
thought she recognized: Kathy thought she had been
transported into a popular TV show of the day called
Romper Room. "I looked around and saw perhaps ten or
twelve other children, all about my age. Some were sitting on the floor and others on wooden benches. In the
front of our group stood a kindly-looking lady with dark
hair tied into a shoulder-length curl. Her face was really
white but, apart from that, she looked just like a schoolteacher. Neatly dressed, plain dark skirt and a blouse.
"As the teacher began talking, I suddenly seemed aware
that I had been here before. The lesson was about how we
are all eternal and live many lives. I heard her say the
word 'reincarnation'." The ghostly teacher chalked a dia-
gram on the classroom's blackboard. "She drew a picture
of what looked like a human being, yet it wasn't. Alongside the misty body, on its left, were bright lines reaching
out towards another, even mistier shape. The teacher told
us that this was our soul and we all moved higher toward
God as we went from life to life. She told us that no one
ever dies; we live forever."

The next day, Kathy did not tell her parents about the
ghostly classroom. She knew they would not believe her.
It was as if the lesson she had learned had to be kept
secret, at least for the time being. Later she thought that
she was being prepared for something. Just months later
the reason became clear.

A family tragedy

Time passed and the year began to die. But the bare branches of the trees in the family garden made Kathy think not of winter, but of spring. Standing alone in the leaf-scattering wind, the five-year-old knew that the end of one year is just the beginning of another. Soon the cold days would pass and once again the trees would bud.

One Saturday morning in January 1960 Kathy was playing in her room when Mr. Stuart came to tell her some terrible news. Geoffrey, Jeanne's five-year-old son, had been hit by a car as he played in the street outside his home. He had been killed instantly.

Kathy's parents drove the 200 miles to their daughter's home in Boston to offer Jeanne their support and love. Of course they took Kathy along. On the day of the funeral, as they filed past little Geoffrey's coffin, Mrs. Stuart told Kathy that he had gone to heaven and would be happy with God. Kathy was about to cry, but suddenly remembered the lesson she had learned in that ghostly classroom just a few months before. She went up to the weeping Jeanne and placed her arms around her neck. "Don't worry," she said. "Geoffrey will soon return."

For a moment all was quiet, then Kathy's parents took her out of the church and told her not to be silly. Geoffrey was, they said, in heaven.

Kathy tried to explain about reincarnation, but no one wanted to listen to her. Even the chaplain spoke to the child, telling her not to say such things. But Kathy was convinced that Geoffrey had simply moved on from his old body and would soon be born again, reincarnated.

That was all almost forty years ago, but to this day Kathy is sure that it is true. When I spoke to her, she told me that she will never forget the white-faced lady she met in that ghostly classroom, nor the lesson she learned there.

Her belief is now that she had sleepwalked into a class held somewhere between this place we call Earth and the next world. And she was certain she had been there before.

ASSESSMENT

Q: Do you think that Kathy was right about the ghostly classroom?

A) The little girl had vivid dreams, that's all.

B) The funeral of the boy her own age upset the five-year-old Kathy, and she comforted herself with the idea of rebirth.

C) As Kathy still believes in the truth of her vision, even after forty years, I don't doubt it either.

Chapter 21

The Haunted
TV Set

Eleanor Fisher is a psychotherapist with a difference. She has a TV set that is tuned to the world beyond. In her office, just outside Boston, Massachusetts, Eleanor advises her clients on their emotional and personal problems. Using her specialist knowledge of human affairs, Eleanor is able to consider their cases and suggest solutions. But when one of her clients presents a really puzzling problem, Eleanor tunes her TV in to the haunted channel. Looking at the screen she can see images and visions of the pathway that her client must take. Eleanor believes her TV set is receiving signals from beyond the grave.

A near-death experience

Eleanor had always been a high achiever, and she had many degrees and qualifications. Her private practice as a therapist was a great success even in the days when her TV set used to receive only the normal broadcasts. But in 1991 she developed a brain tumor, and the surgeon said the only way to save her life was to operate.

This operation was to do far more than save her; it totally changed Eleanor's outlook on life.

As she lay unconscious on the operating table, Eleanor had a strange experience. She became aware that she was no longer in her physical body. Looking down, she could

see the surgeon opening her skull and cutting deep into her brain. But she was not in that body; she was free.

Eleanor felt herself drifting towards a wonderful white light, the like of which she had never seen before. It seemed to be filled with love. A sense of relief flooded through her. If this was death, she thought, then it is a glorious thing. Peace surrounded her, gentle music tinkled in her ears, and in the distance a choir sang some familiar hymn.

Then, from out of the brightness, Eleanor saw her mother and father. They had passed away years before. The thought that her parents were there, waiting to greet her in the next world, caused tears of joy to flood down her cheeks.

"Not yet, Eleanor," her father said. "It's not your time yet."

She did not know what to make of this.

Then her mother spoke. "Go back, Eleanor! There is important work for you there."

When she awoke, her head no longer ached and she felt strangely rested, as though she had enjoyed peaceful sleep rather than major surgery. Her family were there at her bedside. Slowly Eleanor realized that she was back in her physical body, back in the hospital, still alive.

The psychic channel

It took only a short while for Eleanor to recover. She felt bursting with energy. Soon she returned to her practice as a therapist. But something about her had changed.

Eleanor began to notice a new ability to perceive the world differently. It was as if she had X-ray eyes and could visualize the spirits within her clients. She just "knew" what was wrong with them, and she had the power to heal them. To make them whole again.

Shortly after this amazing spiritual awakening, Eleanor discovered that the TV set in her office was tuned in to the world beyond. At first she thought it was a haunted TV. Later she realized that it was she herself who had changed, not the television set.

Eleanor was sitting with a very disturbed client, a young man whose life had been ruined by violent parents. He was crying and pleading with Eleanor to help him put his broken world in order. As she watched the tears flow and heard again his cry for help, Eleanor, almost in tears herself, turned away.

In turning, she caught sight of the TV set standing in the far corner of the room. Oddly there was a program showing. She had been certain it was switched off, but now she couldn't take her eyes off it.

Then she saw the young man on the screen – the person sitting before her. On the TV she saw him working with older people, helping them, caring for them. He looked really happy.

Continuing to watch in utter amazement, Eleanor now saw the scene change to the interior of a church.

There were flowers everywhere. Again she could see the young man, and by his side stood a laughing and lovely young bride.

Eleanor knew at once that she had seen his future, his path to happiness and fulfilment.

Turning back to the still weeping young man, Eleanor told him that his life was not ruined forever. He would live to make something better of it. She told him he would return to college and become a nurse, training to care for older patients. She also assured him that in the future he would meet and marry a beautiful young woman. Eleanor was even able to describe her.

Although it may seem incredible, all that she saw came to be.

Since that day Eleanor Fisher has often used her "haunted" TV set to help clients who are in despair. She is certain that her brain operation opened up an ability within her to see into the future on her very special television set.

ASSESSMENT

Q: Do you believe that Eleanor's TV set is really tuned in to the world beyond?

A) Eleanor only imagines it because her brain is a little damaged.

B) I think Eleanor believes what she says but no TV set can broadcast the future.

C) Eleanor has now got psychic powers and she can see things on the TV screen by using these.

Chapter 22

What Are Ghouls?

Ghouls are particularly nasty types of spooks. It is said that they feast upon human beings. Just as a vampire sucks blood out of a living body, a ghoul sucks out the very energy force of life. Ghouls are the gray ghosts that haunt the edges of darkness between this world and the blackest regions of the next. There are many kinds of ghouls, but all bring misery and suffering to their victims.

So what does a ghoul look like? We don't know, because ghouls are mostly invisible. They are spotted by the feeling of unease that surrounds them. Some describe the feeling a ghoul presence creates as one of great sadness. Others say that it is like being wrapped in a huge, cold, wet blanket, from which there is no escape. Or they can make you tingle inside with fear. It is also believed that some ghouls cause trouble and accidents. Whatever their type, the ghoul is always unpleasant.

Ghouls are sneaky and very mean. They can creep up on you unseen when you enter their lair. Be aware of the signals that a ghoul is around, and leave quickly if you suspect one. That is if you believe in them in the first place, and most people don't.

The good news is that they are quite easy to avoid. Ghouls haunt places and things rather than people. They don't go far from the place that they haunt, so you can just run away, and they won't follow you. The important thing is to know how to spot them. If you come across a place you think may be haunted by a ghoul, apply the Ghoul-Spotting Test on page 106. If the test proves positive, exit quickly and don't look back.

The Ghoulbuster

In the city of Liverpool, made famous by the Beatles, a real-life ghoulbuster can be found. His name is Derek Acorah and he works as a consultant psychic medium from an office in the city center. People from all over the world visit this gifted man to seek guidance from him. But one of Derek's darker duties is to help people whose property and lives are being destroyed by ghosts and ghouls.

The Milky Bar ghoul

One day in February 1998, Derek received a telephone call from a businesswoman named Ann Marie Wright. She said that the nightclub she owned was haunted. When Derek heard the details of the haunting, he immediately agreed to help her. For in Derek's mind, if what Ann Marie said was true, then she and all who entered her club were in terrible danger from a ghoul.

The Milky Bar Club in Wolstenholme Square, central Liverpool, is a swinging disco-dance joint. There young people enjoy loud music and entertainment from early evening to long after midnight. Or they did, until one dark night a ghoul walked in without paying.

The disturbances began in the first week of January 1998. Ann Marie Wright was woken at 5 a.m. by the police, because security alarms at the Milky Bar Club were ringing and only she had the key to turn them off. The police said the premises had been checked and there was no sign of forced entry by a burglar. They drove Ann Marie to the club and it was again checked, both inside and out, but nothing was found.

However, when the police played back the film recorded that night on the internal security video camera, they saw a heavy glass and metal door, leading into the main bar area, open and then close. It looked as though someone had walked through, but there was no one to be seen on the video tape. The club was locked, everything was secure, yet some invisible thing had pushed open that door and entered the bar.

The haunted disco

From that day on the club was haunted by an unseen entity. Glasses would fall from shelves above the bar and smash on the floor. Bottles of beer and wine exploded in their racks and the bottles of spirit started emptying themselves. The bar staff became unnerved by these strange happenings. Some reported feeling a cold, ghostly presence beside them as they served customers. Others became ill. Many said it felt as though all the energy had been drained from their bodies.

There were more problems ahead for the staff and patrons of the Milky Bar Club. One night in late January, for no good reason, many of the customers began to argue and fight with each other. When the security staff had stopped this, they asked those involved what had caused the trouble. No one could offer any explanation. It was a complete mystery. One young man said he felt as if he was being pushed by some unseen force. Another reported feeling dizzy before the fight started. It seemed that something invisible had taken over the customers' minds.

The cleaner's worst challenge

Ann Marie Wright was very concerned about these weird phenomena, which she could not explain. Thinking the problem was centered in the bar area, where the funny occurrences began, she asked the cleaners to give it a good scrubbing and clean-out. Ann Marie had noticed a repulsive funguslike growth that was clinging to the wall behind the bar. It had appeared overnight and hung there like a damp tissue sticking to the plaster. This had to be removed. But doing so made matters worse, much, much worse.

One of the cleaners, Mrs. Vera Jones, a very down-to-earth type, suffered a blow to the head from an unseen hand as she tried to scrub away the strange substance stuck to the wall. She looked round for her attacker, and saw a man's face materialize before her. The eyes seemed to hypnotize Mrs. Jones and she stared at the darkness within them. As the ghostly head floated in front of her, she could see that there was no physical body to support it.

Vera tried to scream. Then the vision of horror opened its mouth and spat at her. The disgusting slime dripped down her face, and its smell made Mrs. Jones feel sick. Quickly she wiped her face, and when she looked up again, the ghastly apparition was gone.

In terror, both of the Milky Bar Club's cleaners ran into the owner's office and insisted that they would not return to their duties until something was done. It was then that Ann Marie decided to contact Liverpool's most famous psychic medium, Derek Acorah.

The ghoul in the gents'

It was raining on the Monday afternoon when Derek and his trusted partner Alan Bates arrived at the Milky Bar Club. As soon as they entered, Derek, sensing the horrible atmosphere, spoke the dreaded word, "ghoul!"

With his highly sensitive psychic powers alert to any sign, Derek began to search for the unseen presence that was haunting this once happy club.

In preparation for the ghoul bust, Alan Bates lit a candle. Its pale flame flickered in the empty club.

A lit candle is customary when ghoulbusting.

"There he is!" Derek had spotted something. He raced

across the dance floor into the gentlemen's lavatory. He had the fiend trapped now! Somewhere in this cold tiled toilet was the ghoul of the Milky Bar Club. Slowly Derek edged forward. Then he saw him.

Crouching down behind a sink in the far corner was a ghostly figure. Derek perceived him as a thin, mean presence and, as he looked closely, he saw that the ghoul's head was almost hanging from his shoulders.

"You will leave this place and go into the light!" Derek said, putting as much firmness and strength into his voice as he could manage.

The ghoul grinned evilly. "Not me!" he said. His half-severed head wobbled sideways as he laughed. "Here I am and here I stay!"

A sickening stink drifted from the unearthly being. Derek coughed in disgust. Alan had followed Derek in and now stood by his side holding out the candle.

"Why are you here?" Derek asked the ghoul.

"I was a sailor visiting this port, when I was murdered by two thieves. They slashed my throat and threw my body into the river Mersey," the ghoul replied.

As Derek looked closely, he could see the gaping wound where the ghost's neck had been cut right down to the gray bone.

Even ghouls have a mother

The air around the ghoul was clammily cold and Derek shivered, but he was not afraid. Well, not very. He closed his eyes and called upon his spirit guide Sam to come and help him. At once the room became warmer.

Derek could see a new shape enter, but this was not Sam. It was the ghost of a woman. She had silvery hair and was dressed in an African shawl.

"I am his mother," said the ghostly figure.

The ghoul stared in disbelief, and so did Derek and Alan.

She reached out her hand and pulled the sorry spectre of her son to her. "We are going now," she whispered softly. Derek saw her turning towards the most beautiful pure white light that had appeared by her side. Without a backward glance, the ghoul and his mother walked forward into eternity.

From that day on the Milky Bar Club has been completely free of ghouls or ghosts. The staff are all happy and no one has reported any strange happenings. Unless you think dancing the lambada is a bit weird.

ASSESSMENT

Q: Why do you think a ghoul would want to haunt a noisy nightclub?

A) Ghouls are imaginary creatures that exist only in people's minds. A nightclub, with its dark corners and dim lights, would be the ideal place for mistaking shadows for spooks.

B) In the story, it says that the ghoul was emptying drinks from behind the bar. Perhaps it was looking for a friendly spirit – whiskey, vodka, or ghoul hooch.

C) Ghouls prey upon people's life forces and a nightclub would have crowds of energetic young people in it. This would be an ideal haunting ground for a greedy ghoul.

Chapter 24

Ghoul-Spotting

The following check list will enable you to examine any area, place, or property where strange happenings have been reported, and determine whether there is the slightest possibility of a ghoul.

To do this properly, you should actually touch the walls or fabric of the area you are searching and feel with your mind. Then refer to the Ghoul Test below. Just place a tick in either Box "A" or Box "B", whichever best describes your feelings about the area you are checking.

The Ghoul Test

NAME OF AREA_____

_____

	A		B
HAPPY	___	SAD	___
WARM	___	COLD	___
COMFORTABLE	___	UNCOMFORTABLE	___
DRY	___	DAMP	___
RELAXING	___	DISTURBING	___
FRIENDLY	___	UNFRIENDLY	___
PEACEFUL	___	RESTLESS	___
LIGHT	___	DARK	___
SMELLS GOOD	___	SMELLS BAD	___
SOUNDS FINE	___	SOUNDS TERRIBLE	___

Total number of ticks in Box "B": _____

8-10: Could be a ghoul here. Do not return to this place without your parent or guardian being with you. Unless of course this is your school. If so, go and see your head ghoulmaster.

6-7: You don't like this place, do you? But it's not very likely that a ghoul is about this area. Even so, stay away if you can. Better safe than sorry.

4-5: Not nice, but nothing like as bad as a ghoul would make it. Incense or candles might help, but be careful not to cause a fire.

1-3: Nowhere is perfect, is it? So change what can be changed and make the best of the rest.

0: Don't know what you were worried about in the first place.

Chapter 25

Spooks – Calling Them Up and Seeing Them Off

Getting rid of unwanted ghosts, ghouls, or the odd pesky poltergeist can be a bit tricky and experts are usually called in. The procedure is often called exorcism, especially if it involves a priest. There have been many horror films made about this subject.

Exorcism of spirits or ghosts has been practised throughout history. Taoist priests in ancient China had a special ritual for it. The priest would dress in a red robe and carry a sword made of the wood from a peach or date tree. An altar would be built in the area where the spirit was supposed to be, and a mystical scroll was burned upon it. This, along with other rites and a few hard words, was thought to drive the ghost away.

In Western tradition too there are magical rituals said to exorcise a ghost. One such involves the drawing of a five-pointed star – a pentagram – in which the exorcist stands. He or she must then call upon the ghost to appear and explain why it is haunting the place. Many spirits are thought to be trying to get a message through to the living. Once they have done this, they can move on to the next world. The exorcist must undertake to pass the spirit's message on in return for the ghost leaving the area in peace.

Then there are those who actively try to get hold of spirits of dead people. The nineteenth-century fashion was to hold a séance. This is a group of people sitting in a circle, trying to contact the dead via a medium. It doesn't necessarily work, though. There's never a spirit when you need one, and then three come along at once.

Who deals with spooks?

exorcist

Someone who performs a ritual of casting or driving out unwanted spirits. This is often a religious function. A Christian exorcist is a priest who calls upon the power of God to banish the spook from the area or person haunted by it.

medium

Someone who claims to be able to communicate with the spirits of the dead. Some mediums also claim to be able to rescue lost ghosts. They believe that ghosts are really spirits of dead people that are trapped between this world and the next. So they call upon higher spirits to come from wherever higher spirits usually hang out, and guide the lost soul to where it's supposed to be.

psychic

Someone who can pick up signals not accounted for by scientific laws.

shaman

In some religions, a kind of priest who goes into a trance in which he or she is believed to communicate with spirits or enter another, supernatural world.

witch

Someone who performs magic. Witches have sometimes also been believed to communicate with ghosts through a familiar spirit. A familiar spirit is a kind of gofer between the witch and the world beyond, and is thought to inhabit the body of an animal. Cats, black dogs, and even frogs feature in the folklore of witchcraft.

In the course of research, the author has met many real witches and none of them looked a bit like the ugly old women witches you see in cartoons.

The Bible tells the story of a certain witch of Endor who had a familiar spirit. King Saul, the first king of Israel, sent for her because he wanted to ask questions about his future. He asked her to conjure up the spirit of the dead King Samuel.

She did so, and the ghost said, "Why have you disquieted me?"

King Saul told the spirit that his enemies were about to attack him.

"As the Lord liveth, ye are worthy to die," the ghost commented.

Sure enough, the Philistines attacked and Saul's army was defeated. The king killed himself. This is what comes of asking ghosts for advice.

The Ghoul of Hell House

Daena Smoller is a senior investigator working with Larry Montz and the International Society for Paranormal Research. It is, says Daena, the most interesting job she has ever done, but it can be extremely scary at times. So I asked her to tell me about the most frightening case she had ever investigated.

Growing pale, she said in a quiet voice, "Without doubt the most terrifying case was the ghoul of Hell House." This is the awful story.

A cry for help

It was early June 1997 and Daena Smoller was the duty investigator answering the telephone at the ISPR head office in Los Angeles. Taking the first call of the day, she heard the voice of a frightened young woman. She said that her home was haunted by a horrible invisible something that had moved into an upstairs room.

It was a cry for help that Daena, on behalf of the ISPR, agreed to answer. Little did she know that this cry for help was soon to turn into a blood-curdling scream.

Daena arranged the details with Dr. Montz and, on a warm summer morning, an ISPR investigation team met to find out whether the home of the scared young woman really was haunted. Dr. Montz himself led the team, which consisted of a psychic medium called Maria Saganis

111

and three ISPR technical investigators: Daena Smoller with the electronic magnetometer, Juliann Meyers with a stills camera, and Steve Ciccone with a video camera. Together they drove into downtown Los Angeles. What they saw and experienced that day changed those brave people forever.

Welcome to Hell House

When Dr. Montz saw the house, he felt uneasy. There was something odd about it. Daena felt it too: "It was like the home of the Munsters! I called it Hell House as soon as I saw it. The windows seemed to be staring at me and the whole building had an air of evil about it."

Juliann insisted on taking photographs before the ISPR team entered. Sinister though the house looks, the pictures gave little clue to the horror that was yet to unfold.

The rusted iron gate at the front of the house squeaked on its hinges as Dr. Montz slowly pushed it open. Inside the creepy-looking house something moved. With almost unbelievable speed, a huge Rottweiler dog charged out of the front door and ran slavering and growling towards them.

"Down, Angel! DOWN!" shouted a voice. Daena recognized it as belonging to the frightened woman who had called her. The huge beast stopped in its tracks, teeth bared and eyes glaring.

Daena and the team looked around them. The front yard was full of rotting metal objects that were twisted into weird shapes.

"My husband is an artist," said the lady from Hell House. "Do you like these? There's lots more inside."

There was something about the woman that Daena did not like one little bit. Glancing over to Maria, the psychic medium, Daena noticed that she had gone very pale, as though she was about to faint.

Entering through the front door, Daena was shocked

112

Hell House, haunted by a Ghoul.

Dr. Larry Montz and Daena Smoller with the Magnetometer inside Hell House.

to see that all the walls had been painted black and covered with mystical signs. The house stank of mould and dirt. It was very cluttered and bits of meaningless ironwork lay scattered everywhere. These twisted metal things were covered in spiders' webs full of dead flies and dust. The place felt as though it had been ruined on purpose.

Juliann, who has nerves of steel, was busy taking photographs. The vile atmosphere had not affected her at all – yet.

Dr. Montz called the ISPR team together. Then he wanted to hear from the inhabitants of the house what they had seen or heard that made them think this place was haunted. No one else lived there, the woman said, except her husband.

Clumping down the rickety wooden staircase came a tall, thin man of about thirty. His bare arms were covered in grime and ended in strong-looking, clawlike hands. "Do you like my work?" he asked, with a sick kind of smile on his sunken face, as he pointed at a twisted chunk of black metal.

No one replied.

The lady of the house introduced her husband and explained that they had both been hurt by a wicked unseen something that had moved into the house.

By now, Maria was almost shaking with fear.

"It's a ghoul!" she said.

Dr. Montz stood firm in the dark and dismal hallway of Hell House. "Let's go find it!" he said.

The ghoul attacks

From room to room the full team of the ISPR went, searching, moving ever upwards towards the highest areas of Hell House, where the lady had said she had been attacked by the invisible presence. Suddenly, as the team entered one of the top-floor rooms, Daena began to feel dizzy and weak, as if something had drained her of energy.

Maria Saganis immediately sensed that the ghoul was present. She tuned in to the psychic wavelength, and within seconds she began to tremble and shake. The room went deathly cold. The others held their breath.

Then Maria opened her mouth and screamed the most blood-chilling scream Daena had ever heard. Looking at her friend, she was appalled to see not Maria but a red-eyed monster. "It was as though Maria had changed into a big, powerful, beastlike man," she told me later. Dr. Montz too was shocked by Maria's transformation into a monster.

"Ha, ha! You get it now!" laughed the creature that only seconds before had been Maria. Its arms lashed out, clawing at the face of Daena, who yelled in terror and jumped backwards.

The lady of the house was screaming now, "It's here! Help, help!" Steve Ciccone and Dr. Montz grabbed the beast that was Maria and held tight.

Suddenly she shuddered in their arms and became herself again. The ghoul had gone.

Maria was in shock. Never in her life as a psychic had she encountered anything so horrible as the ghoul of Hell House. For a few moments that vile, evil entity had taken over her body. Maria trembled and tears ran down her face.

Back downstairs, Dr. Montz questioned the lady and her husband, who admitted that they had been messing with black magic.

The ISPR investigation continued on another day. The final conclusion in Dr. Montz's report was that this foolish young couple had conjured up a long-dead spirit that turned out to be a ghoul. This fiendish ghost had set up home in Hell House and was able to feed on the living energy of anyone who entered there.

And it's still there ...

One thing is for certain, Daena Smoller and Maria Saganis will never again return to face the terror of that evil old mansion. Nor will the young couple; they abandoned the place that they had helped to infest with a ghoul. The building still stands, dark and empty of human life. Now, whatever it is that walks within Hell House, walks alone.

ASSESSMENT

 Q: Do you think that Maria Saganis was really attacked by a ghoul?

A) Not at all. People who call themselves psychic mediums are likely to imagine anything.

B) Most likely the spooky, horrible atmosphere made everyone believe there was a ghoul.

C) Ghouls do prey upon people and it is possible that Maria was attacked by this evil entity.

Chapter 17

Hocus-Pocus

The world of ghosts, ghouls and spirits is full of fakery. In this chapter we will look at some frauds and the way phoney mystics work. No serious investigator of the supernatural believes everything they're told and neither should you.

"Hocus-pocus" is an expression used by jugglers and magicians when they perform a trick by sleight of hand. Here are some of the tricks played on an unsuspecting public by con artists. Perhaps tricks like these work because so many people want to believe in the supernatural.

The Amityville Horror hoax

It is a fact that on November 13, 1974, Ronald Defeo committed six horrible murders in a house on Ocean

Avenue, Amityville, New York. His victims were all family members. He claimed that strange voices in his head had told him to kill. The judge and jury didn't accept this, and he was sent to prison for life. The house was put up for sale.

Owing to its history, the house proved difficult to sell. But eventually it was bought for $80,000 by George and Kathy Lutz. The price was cheap for the area, but even so, George could not really afford it. The bills became too much for him to pay. So, instead of just selling it off, he invented a really spooky story.

There were supposed to be cloven-hoof marks in the snow around the house. Unseen voices were calling out threats, the Lutzes alleged. There were vile smells and lots of flies. The Lutzes also claimed that the house had been built on an old Native American burial site.

This load of jiggery-pokery was made up with help from an established author called Jay Anson, who had helped write the script of the infamous 1973 film *The Exorcist*. Anson never met the Lutzes at all. He didn't even visit Amityville. But he did write a very readable horror story that George and Kathy Lutz said was based on fact.

The book became a best-seller. It was also made into a film. But the entire "Amityville Horror" case was just a huge hoax. People believed it because it was written in a convincing manner, and because they wanted to believe it.

Not one of the local officials mentioned in the book confirms the story told by the Lutz family. For example, the Lutzes never called the police to investigate any strange phenomena at the house. The local priest never entered the building to bless it. And in 1979, while under oath in a court of law, George Lutz admitted that Anson made it all up.

The proceeds from the book and the film ended all the Lutzes' financial problems. They managed to sell the

Amityville house, too. But later they were sued for damages by the people who bought the house. Not because of ghost trouble! The problem was that the book had made it famous. Hordes of people turned up to gawp at the Amityville Horror house. So in a way it ended up being haunted – by the public.

Phoney psychics and spirit mediums

The Western world has many phoney psychics and so-called spirit mediums. They make money by pretending to contact spirits or see the future. The author has met many who seem genuine, but there are many more who are not.

Frauds will say things that are designed to make you think they really are psychic and are tuned in to you and your life. Like Sherlock Holmes, they'll be alert for any clues you give without knowing it – your clothes, the way you speak, and your reactions to what they say. If you go to see a fortuneteller who looks deep into a crystal ball and then says, "I see a classroom …", does that mean they're psychic?

Of course not!

And they will say things that apply to almost anyone. Have you ever read your horoscope in a magazine and thought how well it fitted you? And then noticed you'd read the wrong sign by mistake?

Here are some typical questions used by these frauds to get money from people seeking advice.

Q: Is there a number 3 on your door?

You can't win with this one. If you say no, then the psychic says, "Well, are you one of three …? I can see the number 3 around you." Quite likely there are three people in your family, or your desk at school is third from the window, or your dog is three years old – if they make you think about it long enough, something will fit the number 3.

Q: Do you live on or near a corner?

Of course you do – we all do. But once you have answered yes, you're in their hands and they'll lead you right round the bend.

Q: Why can I see a red car near your house?

Red is the most popular color for cars. Who hasn't got a red car near their house? The phoney mediums who come out with this line deserve a psychic parking ticket.

Q: Whoever owns this red car has been on holiday recently.

And if you say no, they try: "In that case they are just about to go." Well, most people take a holiday once or twice a year, so this is quite likely to fit the red car's owners too.

Q: Has the furniture in your house been moved recently?
It would be a strange household that didn't move the chairs and TV round now and again, wouldn't it?

Q: Have you been feeling unwell lately?
Come on now! Who hasn't had a cold, a tummy upset, or a headache in the last month? Besides, you're obviously worried enough about something to consult a psychic. Perhaps your health is part of the problem.

Q: Someone very close, or is it you, has been reading a book, pages turning?
Isn't this fun? They know so much about you, don't they?

Q: Why can I see an old gentleman with chest trouble?
"Well, fancy that," they're hoping you'll say, "it's my old grandfather." Of course it isn't! It's just in the psychic fraudster's script. But say yes and watch as they clutch their chest and pretend to feel the pain. You might as well enjoy the show; you're paying for it.

Prove it for yourself!

Do you doubt that this script works? Well, go on, try it on your friends! You could even dress up as a fortuneteller at the next bazaar or fête to raise funds for your school or a charity. Maybe ask your clients to shuffle a deck of playing cards and then spread them out in front of you in a mysterious pattern. Pretend to stare at these while you get on with the script. People will think you are a real psychic medium. But don't forget to keep a straight face, that's the trick!

> ## CAUTION!
> Take advice from your parents, teachers, or religious adviser before you even consider talking to anyone who claims to be a psychic, a medium, a fortuneteller, or any such thing. Many people and religions are opposed to the whole idea. At no time should you accept advice from anyone other than people whom you and your advisers trust.

The most haunted house in England?

Borley Rectory once stood on the border between the counties of Essex and Suffolk in southeast England. For years it was thought to be the most haunted house in England.

It was investigated in the 1930s by a ghost-hunter called Harry Price. The spooky phenomena he reported included strange lights, ringing bells, a screaming skull, flying stones, and a phantom monk. You name it, Borley Rectory had it.

Harry Price even claimed it had been built on the site of an old monastery, which was totally untrue.

The books and articles Harry Price wrote about this "most haunted" house made him famous and no doubt quite wealthy too. He was frequently interviewed on the radio and the press published many stories about him and the scary Borley Rectory. But eventually one newspaper sent a journalist to investigate. He found a very different Borley Rectory to the one described by Harry Price.

As part of his research, the journalist, Charles Sutton (no relation to the author), spent a night in Borley Rectory with Harry Price and one of his ghost-hunters. According to Mr. Sutton's report, the night air was indeed filled with odd noises, screeches and scratchings.

So the reporter searched the house for evidence of

ghosts. Suddenly a large pebble struck him on the head. Was it the work of an unseen hand? Mr. Sutton wasn't so easily fooled. He insisted on examining Harry Price's pockets. Sure enough, there were pebbles and stones in them.

Another journalist, Cynthia Ledsham, also interviewed Harry Price at Borley Rectory. She arranged for a photographer to take Mr. Price's picture with the old rectory behind him. When the photograph was developed, it seemed to show a brick flying through the air behind Mr. Price. He claimed it was the world's first photograph of poltergeist activity.

His bluff was easily called. Ms. Ledsham revealed that when the picture was taken, a workman was knocking down a brick wall and had been throwing the bricks into a pile behind Mr. Price.

But if Borley Rectory was not haunted, what had caused those odd noises Mr. Sutton heard? Local people living around Borley Rectory said that there were indeed creepy nonhuman occupants of this supposed haunted house. They were, they reported, rats.

Why bother?

The truth is out there! The problem is that hocus-pocus fraudsters ruin it for real spook-hunters. By making up false ghost stories, tricksters turn what should be properly recorded investigations into a joke. If you are serious about looking into the facts of any haunting, then you must tell only the truth. Do not believe everything you are told, and always ask questions. Be skeptical, but keep an open mind.

Who knows, perhaps you could be the one who finally proves beyond reasonable doubt that ghosts really do exist.

Chapter 28

The Texan
Spooks

In the quaint little town of Claude, near Amarillo, Texas, U.S.A., there lives a family of ghosts: Mom, Dad, and little baby ghost. They share their home with Kristi Beckham, who has seen and heard them ever since she moved in four years ago.

A haunting hillbilly tune

The first odd thing Kristi noticed was that her radio would change stations during a program. One minute she was listening to modern pop songs, the next thing country and western music was playing. Thinking this might just be a fault on her radio, Kristi switched it off and put her favorite singer's latest album in her CD player. Two tracks into this, the CD switched off, and on came some more country and western.

When she went to check how this had happened, Kristi saw a tall, well-built man wearing a Stetson hat. He was standing by her CD machine, tapping his feet in time to the music.

Kristi was shocked. She thought this was someone who had broken in to rob her. She was just about to scream when she saw – though she could hardly believe her eyes – that the tall Texan was disappearing. Slowly his body dissolved into thin air and Kristi could see no trace of him. All that remained was the country music on the radio.

Meet Mrs. Ghost

Some weeks later Kristi was preparing for bed when she looked up to see a beautiful young woman standing near her bedroom door. She knew this was not a real live person because the figure had no feet. It seemed to float above the floor.

Suddenly Kristi saw the ghostly woman's eyes flash red. She looked really angry. Yet Kristi knew she would not hurt her, and she remained calm. When she looked again, the ghost had gone.

Starting a family

Over the last four years Kristi has seen the tall, male Texan ghost many times. He is always playing tricks with the radio and TV, switching channels to programs with a Western theme. John Wayne movies seem to be his favorite. Whenever one of these is broadcast, the TV switches itself to that channel.

Recently Kristi has begun hearing the sound of a baby crying in the night. She has

never seen the child but her cats Mouser and Puddles seem to be able to. Whenever Kristi hears the invisible baby cry, she sees her two pets sitting together staring at thin air.

Kristi Beckham is not afraid of her Texan spooks, and they are obviously not frightened of her. They must be quite happy to have set up home alongside her, and now they have a new ghost baby to complete their unearthly family. Perhaps the cowboy ghost will turn down his country songs to let the spooky child sleep. Kristi hopes so – she can't stand hillbilly music!

ASSESSMENT

Q: What do you think Kristi should do?

A) Kristi's tuner is drifting, and so is her mind! She should get a grip.

B) Kristi should get her equipment checked, and her eyes too. And find out who lived in the house before her – just in case.

C) If you can't lick 'em, join 'em! Kristi should take up line dancing, and they could all dance together to the haunting hillbilly music.

Chapter 29

Final Assessment

Mainly As

Your scientific mind refuses to accept that ghosts and ghouls exist outside the imagination of human beings. You do not believe in haunted houses, poltergeists, or any kind of supernatural happening. To you, if a thing cannot be measured, weighed, tested, and examined, then it is unworthy of consideration. Even seeing an apparent ghost would not make you doubt the hard and fast rules of physics that deny the possibility of spooks. You believe that sightings of ghosts can be explained away as hallucinations or hocus-pocus trickery. As for spook stories, well, you think they're just kids' stuff. For your birthday you want a telescope, because if there are any unexplained beings to be found, they are in outer space.

Mainly Bs

You would like to believe in ghosts and hope that one day you may see one. In the meantime you are thinking very carefully about the whole subject of unexplained happenings. Your mind isn't made up one way or the other. You are still open to arguments for and against. Perhaps you'll have a go at hunting for a spook and if you find one, then you will believe.

However, you are not so sure about the truth of spooky stories, though you enjoy reading them. You always weigh things up before you make any decision and will not be rushed when doing so. For your birthday you haven't decided what you want, but you are certain to get it.

Mainly Cs

You really do believe in spooks, don't you? And why not? The world would be a very dull place if there weren't a few of us around. You may already have seen a ghost; even if you haven't yet, you will one day. And don't worry: it will recognize that you're a friend. Treat it politely and don't forget to make a note of what it has to say. When you take part in a ghost hunt, you are certain to be the psychic investigator, tuning in to the world beyond. For your birthday you want a magnetometer and a haunted mansion to hunt spooks in. Whoooo! Look out behind you!